◆◆◆

THE HARLEM RENAISSANCE AND THE IDEA OF A NEW NEGRO READER

◆◆◆

A VOLUME IN THE SERIES
Studies in Print Culture and the History of the Book

EDITED BY
Greg Barnhisel
Robert A. Gross
Joan Shelley Rubin
Michael Winship

THE HARLEM RENAISSANCE
AND THE IDEA OF A NEW NEGRO READER

SHAWN ANTHONY CHRISTIAN

UNIVERSITY OF MASSACHUSETTS PRESS
Amherst and Boston

Copyright © 2016 by University of Massachusetts Press
All rights reserved
Printed in the United States of America

ISBN 978-1-62534-201-0 (paper); 200-3 (hardcover)

Designed by Sally Nichols
Set in Adobe Minion Pro and Berthold Walbaum
Printed and bound by Sheridan Books, Inc.

Cover design by Jack Harrison
Cover art: *Staff of* The Messenger *in the magazine's offices*. Frank R. Crosswaith Photograph Collection, 1920s. Photographs and Prints Division, Schomburg Center for Research in Black Culture, The New York Public Library, Astor, Lenox and Tilden Foundations

Library of Congress Cataloging-in-Publication Data

Names: Christian, Shawn Anthony, author.
Title: The Harlem Renaissance and the Idea of a New Negro Reader / Shawn Anthony Christian.
Description: Amherst : University of Massachusetts Press, 2016. | Series: Studies in print culture and the history of the book | Includes bibliographical references and index.
Identifiers: LCCN 2016012905| ISBN 9781625342010 (pbk. : alk. paper) | ISBN 9781625342003 (hardcover : alk. paper)
Subjects: LCSH: African Americans—Books and reading—History—20th century. | American literature—African American authors—History and criticism. | Harlem Renaissance. | African Americans in literature. | Harlem (New York, N.Y.)—Intellectual life.
Classification: LCC Z1039.B56 C47 2016 | DDC 028/.908996073—dc23 LC record available at https://lccn.loc.gov/2016012905

British Library Cataloguing-in-Publication Data
A catalog record for this book is available from the British Library.

◀▶◆◀▶

For my students then, now, and in the future
And
To the memory of my grandparents, Vondra Russell, James Brown,
Louise Sherrod, and Sylvia and Henry Christian

◀▶◆◀▶

CONTENTS

Acknowledgments
ix

Introduction. The New Negro Is Reading
1

1. Creating Critical Frameworks
Three Models for the New Negro Reader
16

2. In Search of Black Writers (and Readers)
Crisis's and Opportunity's *Literary Contests*
42

3. Beyond *The New Negro*
Artistry, Audience, and the Harlem Renaissance Literary Anthology
68

4. Pedagogy for Critical Readership
James Weldon Johnson's English 123
94

Epilogue. On African American Writers and Readers
115

Notes
121

Index
137

ACKNOWLEDGMENTS

The journey to complete this book has fortunately included many people. My colleagues, friends, and family have been unselfish with their time, positive energy, patience, and love. I made my way to this point and to this now tangible labor of love only because they have been and remain a tremendous community of support. I am eternally indebted to each of them.

I am especially grateful for the inspiration and flexibility that my colleagues and students at Wheaton College in Norton, Massachusetts, have afforded me over the course of this journey. The support of my English department colleagues has been invaluable—my sincere thanks to each of them! A special thank you as well to my SILCS family; I honor the journey that each of them will undertake. In the form of time and research support, I cannot thank Wheaton College enough for helping to make a long-held interest in the Harlem Renaissance much more concrete.

This book would not have the focus and form it does without the opportunities afforded me by the Burton Historical Collection at the Detroit Public Library, the Center for Ethnic Studies and the Arts at the University of Iowa, the Manuscript and Rare Books Library at Emory University, the Beinecke Rare Book and Manuscript Library at Yale University, the Rockefeller Library at Brown University, the Wallace Library at Wheaton College, and the Schomburg Center for Research in Black Culture of the New York Public Library. At each of these sites, I was welcomed, cared for, and affirmed. Through them, I also came to know the Harlem Renaissance better and developed a real appreciation for its enduring character.

I sincerely thank the staff at the University of Massachusetts Press,

ACKNOWLEDGMENTS

especially Brian Halley, Carol Betsch, Mary Bellino, Amanda Heller, and Karen Fisk, and for their steadfast work on this book and Steven Moore for the index. I was fortunate to have their patience, flexibility, and care throughout this process—again, thank you! My thanks as well to the anonymous reviewers for their sound feedback and compelling recommendations.

I am fortunate to have as standard-bearers, colleagues, and friends some of the brightest minds and most dedicated scholars working today. I humbly thank Gillian Johns, William James, Chantalle Verna, Ayesha Hardison, Sam Moody, Reginald A. Wilburn, Kate Capshaw Smith, Cassie Steele, Joycelyn Moody, Warren Carson, Daniel Scott, Charles Wilson, and Cheryl Wall for their generous feedback and encouragement. Because their guiding hands enabled this journey, I remain grateful for the opportunity that Marlon Ross, Anne Ruggles Gere, Carla O'Connor, and Alford Young Jr. gave to me so many years ago: "no matter how high I get / I'll still be looking up to you!"

For allowing me to learn from and grow with them over so many years, I lovingly thank Steven Gillespie, Rey Lopez, James Melton, James and Joshua Frazier, Steven Jones, Odis Johnson, Tehani Collazo, LaTissia Mitchell, Judy, Millery, and Ellison Polyné, Harley Etienne, R. Scott Heath, Kimberly and Yohance Murray, Stan Adams, Michael Powell, Keisha Ferguson and William (Tre) Gray, Ravi Perry, Kenyatta Graves, Seth Cosimini, Afua Akoto, Samantha Andreacchi, Nell Smith, Randy Frazer, Shane Nichols, Catherine Braxton, and Luis Paredes: I am so fortunate that each of them keeps me right and connected to the world through their phone calls, texts, and visits. Thank you for each and every one! I must extend an extra-special thank you to my "partner in crime" Marcus Allen; his love, friendship, and humor made so much possible.

Providence, Rhode Island, is intimately tied to this book. I am grateful to that city for its charm and beauty, and for nurturing the true friendships I have with the finest human beings on this planet: Alex Vasquez, Claudia and Mark Mathis, Monica Key, Derek Doura, Garrick (Lamont) Combs, Kelly Rose Belanger, Paul Kieltyka, Cherie Small, Christano, Michelle, and Lauren Andrade, Philly Baut, Dimitry, Israel, and Josue Anselme, Pamela Donaldson, T'Sey-Haye Preaster, Sean Kelly, Dennis

ACKNOWLEDGMENTS

and Ana-Cristina Montalvo, Kyle Pereria, Justin Russillo, Kevin Harrison-Lombardi Jr., Manu Platt, Lee Harris, Stephen and Sarah Mathis, Jessica Lopez, Justin Nicoll, Andres and Jose Ruiz, Josh Child, Peter Deffet, Shauna Turner, Colin Channer, and the staff and board members of the Rhode Island Council for the Humanities. I thank each of them for making Providence home for me. And finally, being in Providence has come to mean so much more because it brought Keota Fields and me together. I am truly blessed to have him—my brother, colleague, and friend—in my life.

My family—the Browns, Christians, Hudsons, Jordans, Sanders, and Vickers—has always supported and loved me through everything. I could not ask for more than that. I praise God for them! I thank my parents, Christal Brown Jordan and Cartha Christian, for the good counsel, rich laughter, and unwavering love. I thank my siblings, Ariel, Cartha (Joe), Dakota (Kody), Keota, and Taurus, for reminding me to live the good life and allowing me still to be a "big brother." Thank you, Taurus Jr., Laila, Terrell, Tanyiah, and Trinity—an uncle's dream—for the sheer and utter joy! Thanks as well to my "team" of aunts, uncles, and cousins from Florida to California. Their energy and presence give me so much strength!

THE HARLEM RENAISSANCE AND THE IDEA OF A NEW NEGRO READER

INTRODUCTION
The New Negro Is Reading

◁◆◁

On page three of its May 1919 issue, the Chicago-based *Half-Century* magazine celebrated "every colored person that [could] read" with the article "The New Negro Is Reading."[1] The article's unnamed author—quite probably *Half-Century*'s pioneering publisher and editor Kathryn Williams-Irwin—described reading experiences throughout African America in the context of World War I. She found that "those who were accustomed to reading nothing found their appetites for this knowledge satiated by reading newspapers diligently; those who previously read newspapers sought the higher grade of literature and accuracy [of] the magazine. Those who read magazines stepped further up the ladder of literature to books."[2] Generalizing for effect, this writer's description of progressive reading practices in the midst of the New Negro era (1890–1940) underscored the fact that African Americans were reading widely: newspapers, magazines, and journals as well as books. This self-referential characterization acknowledged the crucial role that the increasingly available print culture played in cultivating African Americans into a readership. For *Half-Century*, a significant segment of that readership was Chicago's black population.

Half-Century began publishing in 1916 and was one of several periodicals to move quickly from local to national visibility. A collaboration between Williams-Irwin and Anthony Overton, who was proprietor of Overton Hygienic Company, *Half-Century* mirrored the lives and interests

INTRODUCTION

of Chicago's black, especially middle-class, residents. The May 1919 issue did so explicitly through the article "The Negro and the Photo-Play" by entrepreneur and filmmaker Oscar Micheaux; popular writer Anita Scott Coleman's short story "Love's Power"; pictures of a prominent baseball hero, Leland Giants and Chicago American Giants outfielder J. "Pete" Hill; and advertisements that featured products such as a "tri-ad switch," or hair extension, from the local Winona Hair Emporium. It also featured associate editor Howard A. Phelps's "Negro Life in Chicago," a series of snapshots that prefigured the exhaustive research on African Americans' social, economic, and political conditions in Chicago that would later be published by St. Clair Drake and Horace Cayton in *Black Metropolis*.[3] Phelps's overview opened with reference to a "pioneer[ing] Chicagoan [who] was a Negro of distinct racial features," Jean Baptiste Point du Sable, invoking Point du Sable's primacy to frame an account of how African Americans' migration to Chicago resulted in the society that "Negro Life in Chicago" chronicled.[4] According to Phelps's reading, black Chicago's interlocking institutions functioned as necessary responses to racism but thrived because of their patrons' relative gains in education, wealth, and political position.

Reflecting on similar social progress among black women, *Half-Century* sketched this scenario in its 1919 commentary about reading in African America: "We often question why so many men and women push ahead so rapidly in worldly affairs; why a certain lady behaves so beautifully, feels at home in any society; why she seems so well informed on what is happening in this world, why she discharges her domestic duties with such ease and ability. Our answer is that she has found the better way. She has been drinking at the fountain of literature." Offering this depiction of middle-class African American womanhood, the writer asserts, from the perspective of an "appreciative reader," that "the *Half-Century Magazine* is the freshest in the literary life of the race." In this way, any reader who identified with this portrait was encouraged to view *Half-Century*, with an estimated average circulation of sixteen thousand throughout its publication period, as indispensable to her efforts to become a reader of literature. Such a reader would likely be willing to contribute "$1.00 [for the] yearly subscription."[5] Recognizing and celebrating the presence of African American readers and literature had the potential to provide mutual benefits.

Half-Century's writer was not alone, of course, in identifying specific African Americans' participation in the "literary life of the race," which included Jessie Fauset's and Countee Cullen's debut works, *There Is Confusion* and *Color*, awards ranging from literary prizes offered by *Crisis* and *Opportunity* to Guggenheim fellowships, and artistic collaborations such as *FIRE!!*[6] Textual exhortations like "The New Negro Is Reading" marked the confluence of an increased circulation of print material, literature especially, and a growing body of African American readers. This explicit consideration of African Americans as readers sought to cultivate within the larger African American population an interest in and skills for reading the literature of the period. In *The Harlem Renaissance and the Idea of a New Negro Reader*, I consider how this composite projection of ideal, intended, and actual readers was deployed to construct an African America reading public.

Among the important changes in African American life that many consider hallmarks of the era, three in particular fueled consideration of a New Negro reader throughout the Harlem Renaissance: literacy gains, a thriving press, and a more tangibly recognized literature. Given the social and legal obstacles and racial violence prohibiting opportunities to read for nearly three centuries, to produce a (more) literate African America in the early years of the twentieth century was a tremendous feat. With the 8 percent drop in African American illiteracy from a reported 30.9 percent in 1910 to 22.9 percent by 1920, the development of New Negro readership was clearly under way.[7] At 288 publications with a combined circulation totaling 500,000 by 1910, the African American press not only supported African Americans' literacy but also served as a major conduit for participation in organizations such as the National Association of Colored Women and the National Urban League; communities that included residents who were also congregants in the African Methodist Episcopal Church; college literary clubs and journals such as Howard University's *Stylus;* and discussions supported by columns and articles in periodicals such as *The Negro World*.[8] The period's newspapers and journals enabled African Americans' development of cultural literacy both public and private.

The Detroit Study Club was representative of sites that cultivated

INTRODUCTION

African American readers' interaction with the print culture of the day. Originally named the Browning Study Club when it began in 1898, the Detroit Study Club was organized by black women, "primarily for the study of the poetry of Robert Browning and for the self-culture of its members."[9] In later years, the study club's interests reflected an increased racial awareness within black civil society, or the "set of institutions, communication networks, and practices that facilitated responses to economic and political challenges confronting black people."[10] In 1925–26, a particularly vibrant year for Harlem Renaissance activity, monthly topics included "notes from N. A. A. C. P. Convention" and "Negro Poets and Their Poems."[11] Victoria Wolcott has argued that "as more African American authors were published during the Harlem Renaissance, clubwomen combined their intellectual work with a sense of racial identity and consciousness. Through reading Jessie Fauset, Zora Neale Hurston, and other African American female authors, these women defined themselves simultaneously as 'race women' and educated members of the middle class."[12] The exclusionary practices of sites such as the American Negro Academy and white women's groups reinforced the need for this identity formation, which moved groups such as the Detroit Study Club into a "distinctly feminized sphere" where black women "encouraged one another to articulate new ideas, support their interpretations, write their own words, and critique one another."[13]

As it did for these clubwomen, the period's literature served as a catalyst for a range of African Americans' cultural practices ranging from leisure activities to intellectual development and circumscribed public debate. In describing readers whose collective relations to print culture constitute what Benedict Anderson described as an "imagined community," Catherine Squires has pointed out that "black people nationwide read [and heard read] the same news of Black accomplishment, outrage, and creativity. The widespread involvement of people of so many different ideological and professional backgrounds enhanced the sense of a national black consciousness, which was truly community based as so many folks from different walks of life contributed to the creation and success of Black papers."[14] An important component of the creativity featured in the press was the increased production of texts authored by

African Americans for individual and collective review. The appearance of early works such as Paul Laurence Dunbar's volume of poetry *Oak and Ivy* and Pauline Hopkins's first novel, *Contending Forces,* followed by the success of James Weldon Johnson's *Autobiography of an Ex-Coloured Man,* Jean Toomer's *Cane,* and Langston Hughes's *Weary Blues,* can be attributed in part to both an increasingly receptive publishing industry and a growing number of venues, such as literary clubs, where African Americans could read such books.[15]

When Charles Chesnutt lent his celebrity and his critical insight to the National Buy-a-Book Campaign in the Interest of Negro Literature in 1916, he was speaking directly to both African American writers and readers, underscoring their roles in furthering this literary production. In his speech "The Negro in Books," Chesnutt encouraged authors to "write such books and create such characters by building up a reading public among ourselves who will buy such books." Chesnutt acknowledged that African Americans were increasingly in a position to read and purchase books that they "would like to have written about them." He supported African American book-buying as one way—an important way—to marry the idea that "colored people should show appreciation for those of their own number" with the necessity of "writing good books about the Negro."[16] *Half-Century*'s article "The New Negro Is Reading" echoed Chesnutt in intimating that because the phenomenon of black people reading (and learning to read) was as palpable as the related print culture that supported it, the early years of the Harlem Renaissance were cause for celebration but also further cultivation. These related dynamics propelled the public dialogue that writers carried on with their readers about what it meant, in Countee Cullen's words, "to make a poet black / and bid him sing!"—to read literature, African American literature, as an art and an exhibition of racial pride.[17]

Though an important component of racial discourse during the Harlem Renaissance, an explicit focus on African Americans as readers, not surprisingly, was often subsumed within efforts to court a white reading public, such as those offered by Alain Locke in his seminal book *The New Negro.* In the preface to the volume, Locke argued that "immediate hope rests in the revaluation by white and black alike of the Negro in terms of

INTRODUCTION

his artistic endowments and cultural contributions, past and prospective. The great social gain in this is the releasing of our talented group from the arid fields of controversy and debate to the productive fields of creative expression. The especially cultural recognition they win should in turn prove the key to that revaluation of the Negro which must precede any considerable betterment of race relationships."[18] Just as several of his contemporaries did through their writings, here Locke defined the New Negro and read its manifestation in a literary (and visual and performing arts) renaissance that had the potential to combat racial prejudice, reverse discriminatory policies, and lead to (modest forms of) integration. Although Locke identified a need for "white *and* black alike" to transform their negative perceptions of African Americans, the potential effect of such racial uplift on whites was a consistent, overarching theme in the way Locke and others named and nurtured the period's literature. Such a focus marginalized the ability of the work, especially of African American poets, novelists, and playwrights, to enact a parallel transformation among African Americans themselves.

In *The Harlem Renaissance and the Idea of a New Negro Reader*, I counter this historic marginalization. The book poses and answers specific questions about the cultivation of African Americans as readers during the Harlem Renaissance, informed by methods of analysis from literacy, reader response, and print culture studies as well as histories of racial uplift and modernism: What do projections of a New Negro reader reveal about the African Americans whom Harlem Renaissance writers targeted? How do such ideas function as evidence for the way African Americans read? Why was outreach to African Americans as literary readers both necessary and possible? And, ultimately, how did Harlem Renaissance writers promote their ideas, and what models for reading did they argue through them? These questions, and the analysis I undertake to answer them, place this book within a growing scholarly effort to complicate and expand our understanding of "New Negro politics," what Henry Louis Gates and Gene Andrew Jarrett argue is "a paradigm encapsulating black and white interest in the cultural politics and the political culture of racial representation."[19] In doing so, I challenge the more dominant characterization of the Harlem Renaissance as solely dependent on the intercultural exchanges among black promoters, black writers, and white patrons.

Scholarly consideration of the Harlem Renaissance as a dynamic culture of print *and* of African American readers has increased in recent years, especially through the work of scholars such as Caroline Goeser, James Danky, and Leon Jackson.[20] Before them, however, there were important treatments, especially Theodore Vincent's *Voices of a Black Nation* and Abby Johnson and Ronald Johnson's *Propaganda and Aesthetics*. Though not framed as print culture histories, each instructively positions print as an essential site of the Harlem Renaissance's cultural work. As a documentary history of how "the 'New Negroes' of the [Harlem] Renaissance seized the opportunity to transform the black press" in the former and an explication of how "the literary materials in Afro-American magazines of the twentieth century weave into a rich narrative" in the latter, both works contributed useful information about the Harlem Renaissance's relationship to the larger question that Danky posed as part of his contribution to *A History of the Book in America*: "What, then, is African American print culture?" While the answer is expansive and includes the "torrent of articles, books, essays, letters, edited works, and more" that Danky enumerates, a central component of that definition is surely the ways in which African Americans use print.[21] In this regard, in *The Harlem Renaissance and the Idea of a New Negro Reader* I undertake a study of Harlem Renaissance print culture from the point of view that, as Carl Kaestle and Janice Radway advocate, "writers and readers were both 'users' of print culture in that they sought to employ magazines, books, and newspapers to accomplish particular ends—that is, to address others, to learn, to constitute a sense of self, or to express beliefs."[22]

Indeed, in their cultivation of a New Negro reader, Harlem Renaissance writers operated similarly, especially in the ways they aligned the public discussion which constituted that effort with the identity expression and related cultural citizenship that many advocated. Given such dynamics, this book positions those writers' concerted hailing of a New Negro reader—from calls for cultural partnership to promotion of the latest works emerging from their contemporaries—as the forging of an interpretive community. Interpretive communities, as Stanley Fish has contended, are "made up of those who share interpretive strategies not for reading (in the conventional sense) but for writing texts, for constituting their properties and assigning their intentions. In other words, these strategies exist prior to the act of reading and therefore determine the shape of what is read."[23]

Across articles and columns about, and even book advertisements for, the period's literature in popular periodicals such as *Crisis* as well as the structure and overall editorial imprint of anthologies such as the celebrated volume *The New Negro*, Harlem Renaissance writers signaled their literature's potential to elicit racial pride and mirror African Americans' changing place within the nation. In addressing and constructing African Americans as New Negro readers, these writers hoped to move them from a basic to a more nuanced cultural literacy. Such development would facilitate critical interpretation of racial representation and artistry, which were essential, many argued, to any New Negro reading experience. In contrast to the New Negro reader that these characteristics described, who was projected as educated and middle class (or aspiring to such socioeconomic status) but in need of the reading guidance that many Harlem Renaissance writers encouraged, the period's actual readers reflected the heterogeneity of African America.[24]

Building, then, on an aim that Lara Langer Cohen and Jordan Stein posit for *Early African American Print Culture*, this book "demonstrates the uneven ways in which print culture enables the coexistence of historical subjects and rhetorical figures."[25] Though not a comprehensive recovery of the practices of more typical African American readers during the period, *The Harlem Renaissance and the Idea of New Negro Reader* engages the unevenness that operates in the gap between rhetorical analysis and reading history which Leon Jackson ascribes to scholarship on African American reading acts.[26] It does so, first, as a response to Elizabeth McHenry's important contention that "inquiry into the history of black readers is further complicated by the difficulty of tracking down evidence of so elusive a practice as reading."[27] Even more, my analyses center on the idea of a New Negro reader invoked by specific writers, often as readers themselves, and when feasible juxtapose the perspectives of other readers. To do so is to "[treat] as intertwined the question of how we conceive of [historical] readers and [their] reading practices, and how empirically we can reconstruct the communities of which they were members."[28]

The idea of a New Negro reader that was promulgated throughout the Harlem Renaissance was indeed more a record of rhetorical gestures than of documented exchanges with actual readers about their literacy practices in general and the personal benefits of reading the period's literature in particular. Nevertheless, it was also instrumental both in circulating that literature and as evidence of the identity (re)formation on which projections of the New Negro depended.[29] As Davarian Baldwin has argued: "New Negroes were identified by the explicit, and sometimes competing, principles of racial uplift, race consciousness, self-determination, and even self-defense as part of a larger international that described themselves as the 'darker races.' . . . As an ideal of race consciousness and self-determination, the New Negro represents a moment in time more so than a discrete collection of individuals who thought and acted the same way. In this moment, there were critical points when individual desires lined up but also could never match up with the collective aims of the New Negro moment."[30] At times both the provocation for enacting these principles and evidence that they had been made real, Harlem Renaissance literature developed within and because of the vicissitudes of the New Negro moment that Baldwin aptly described.

African Americans' interactions with Harlem Renaissance literature were facilitated in and through the period's newspapers, journals, and anthologies, which targeted and thereby cultivated the New Negro as a culturally informed reader. Because, of course, no one single way of reading as a New Negro could ever be realized, the varied ideas about what it meant to read as a New Negro rendered the Harlem Renaissance a period when different "interpretive strategies [were] always being deployed."[31] Such ideas about a New Negro reader served as markers of community, if only in formation, and especially of Harlem Renaissance writers and the other African Americans they targeted. As Benedict Anderson reminds us, "communities are to be distinguished, not by their falsity/genuineness, but by the style in which they are imagined."[32] I read as a style the rhetorical, personality-driven, and often pedagogical work of Harlem Renaissance writers to promote as a tradition texts that were both of high literary quality and racially affirming. As I illustrate in this volume, the implicit and explicit configuration of a New Negro reader in the period's print culture reflected, as Molly Travis has posited about the modernist period more generally, the "cultural effort" that went into making the Harlem Renaissance and its literature "readable."[33]

Elizabeth McHenry has usefully examined communal opportunities to read as important social practices in African American life, arguing, "Reading and responding, whether orally or in writing, to a variety of texts, analyzing ideas, and speaking critically and succinctly in conversation with others were talents deemed essential not only to the advancement of individuals but to the prosperity of the nation as well."[34] Karla Holloway made a related observation in *Book Marks: Reading in Black and White,* where she noted, "Blacks in the United States developed an intimate relationship to books because of the way books came to personify a story of race."[35] Historically, then, reading has always mattered in African Americans' experiences. Despite a long-standing perception that the Harlem Renaissance in general, and its literature in particular, were, as W. E. B. Du Bois once argued, "for the benefit of white people and at the behest of white readers," recent scholarship has compelled rereadings of the period for the ways in which African Americans benefited more directly from the period's literary production.[36]

For example, Michelle Phillips and Belinda Wheeler have attended to the role of print in furthering reading practices in African America at the time. In detailing how Du Bois employed *Crisis* to offer "guided exposures" for its African American readers, children especially, and how Gwendolyn Bennett's *Opportunity* column "Ebony Flute" brought together African America's "geographically displaced readers," Phillips and Wheeler have provided, respectively, further evidence of the collaborative ways that readers experienced Harlem Renaissance literature and the roles of the period's writers in facilitating those interactions.[37] Whether by making books of literary quality about African America (more) available, modeling how to read literature, or enlisting financial support for various publications, Harlem Renaissance writers fashioned the ideal of a New Negro reader as much as they targeted, even spoke directly to, actual readers. This meant writing to African American readers as a diverse group, ranging from black clubwomen to Pullman porters, all responding to the latest reviews in the *Chicago Defender*. Those readers also included young people from Harlem to Atlanta hoping to find their graduation pictures in *Crisis*'s education number. Importantly Harlem Renaissance writers' ideas about a New Negro reader developed at a moment when African Americans were experiencing increased mobility, improved resources, and relatively easier access to goods and services.

Amy Jacques Garvey projected one such image of a New Negro reader in a 1927 editorial for the Universal Negro Improvement Association's (UNIA) *Negro World*. Titled "Read, Think, Then Talk," Garvey's editorial furthered the public discourse about African Americans' reading practices to which *Half-Century* and other periodicals were contributing. "The average Negro has not yet learned," Garvey argued, "the value of good books." This was the case, she observed, despite a context of relative economic stability. "Take Chicago, New York, Philadelphia and Cleveland," she continued, "cities where the average Negro lives at a fairly high standard, which is chiefly due to the credit system. His home or apartment has a parlor which is not completely furnished unless it has a player-piano, Victrola, banjo and ukulele, but never a bookcase, and rarely one finds a single book of readable worth. Occasionally a detective story, Snappy Stories, or *True Romance* magazine, but how can a young race thrive on such drivel?"[38]

With this pointed critique of African Americans' spending habits and cultural leanings, Garvey did more than criticize an overemphasis on "home furnishings" and the taste for popular fiction. She saw them as diminishing the opportunity for intellectual development. Garvey condemned African American readers for limiting themselves to light fiction rather than expanding their knowledge by engaging critical perspectives on the world in which they lived. Popular consumer-based readings fell short of the kind of advancement that the UNIA advocated for African Americans and for blacks throughout the world. In taking every opportunity to read and discuss "good literature," Garvey urged her readers, "you will be benefited, and your race, too, by being able to measure up intellectually with other people."[39]

In the context of *Negro World*'s role in cultivating the period's arts

INTRODUCTION

and letters, Garvey's statements implied that to read such publications was not just a means to learn more about the inherent talents of African America, particularly through literary expression, but a way to see, read, and become part of an entire "Negro world" in the making.[40] As Garvey addressed the choices made by African Americans as social agents, her concerns stemmed from the premise that what and how one read dictated how one behaved socially, politically, and fiscally. Ultimately, Garvey's comments were aimed at shaping the consumers that a larger number of African Americans were becoming. In detailing her perspective on the practices of "average" readers who were frequently described as disadvantaged equally by limited resources and reading experiences, Garvey underscored that reforming African Americans' reading practices, and the way they spent their money in general, was far from a simple matter of racial uplift. With "wage-earning blacks," as Susannah Walker has noted, "generally [having] more expendable income than their rural counterparts" and "life in the city [requiring] greater engagement with consumer culture than did life in the country" throughout the second decade of the twentieth century, Harlem Renaissance writers often promoted their notions about an African American reading public in terms of class.[41] Indeed, their comments increasingly claimed that a majority of African America, especially its middle classes, would benefit just as much as their white counterparts from guidance in how to be, in the words of Sterling Brown, "a reading folk."[42]

To trace this development, the chapters of *The Harlem Renaissance and the Idea of a New Negro Reader* begin in 1919 with the tangible turn to the Harlem Renaissance and then move chronologically through to the early 1930s, when "rebellion against the Civil Rights Establishment [surged] on the part of many of the artists and writers whom the Establishment had assembled and promoted."[43] Specifically, in the first two chapters I consider the ways in which some Harlem Renaissance writers model versions of a New Negro reader—first as a close reader and then as a potential writer. The third chapter shows how writer-centered orientations to reading operate in the anthology, arguably the Harlem Renaissance's most resounding literary artifact. The fourth chapter provides a related look at how the practices of Harlem Renaissance writers and readers structure formal education. Running throughout this group of specific but related texts and contexts making up Harlem Renaissance print culture is, then, a rich narrative that details the idea of a New Negro reader.

Displaying their "close reading" of the period's literature was an important way that Harlem Renaissance writers achieved this cultural production. Often presented in book reviews and more general essays that complemented sections of poetry and serialized fiction in journals such as *Crisis* and newspapers such as the *Pittsburgh Courier,* these close readings constituted moments when writers quoted or referred to a passage from a given work and then analyzed it as representative of that work's overall value, which, in the context of the Harlem Renaissance, was commonly measured in terms of how a work depicted African American life.

James Weldon Johnson, Jessie Fauset, and Sterling Brown were readers and writers of Harlem Renaissance literature whose documented cultural literacies in this regard circulated among many African Americans. Chapter 1, "Creating Critical Frameworks," analyzes representative instances of their literary criticism. In Johnson's *Book of American Negro Poetry,* Fauset's book reviews in *Crisis,* or Brown's columns in *Opportunity,* African American readers encountered related but sometimes contrasting images of a New Negro reader, which had potential as models, even tools, for shaping their own experiences with the period's literature.

Just as influential as readers as they were as writer-editors, W. E. B. Du Bois and Charles S. Johnson launched and oversaw literary contests that positioned African American readers as promising writers, or at least as having the potential to become so. Chapter 2, "In Search of Black Writers (and Readers): *Crisis*'s and *Opportunity*'s Literary Contests," explores these contests for the ways that they, too, constructed but also furthered the idea of a New Negro reader. Through the contests, Harlem Renaissance writers targeted other black readers as partners in developing the best writing about and from African America. Although, between the two journals, only six major contests were held over a three-year period, from 1925 to 1927, *Crisis* and *Opportunity* garnered a great deal of visibility for emerging writers and made the contests central in African American

INTRODUCTION

life. As a result, their literary contests came to play an essential role in the way the Harlem Renaissance functioned as, to borrow from Nathan Huggins, a "public relations promotion."[44] Because they were literary features, these contests also indicate how Harlem Renaissance writers augmented their visions of other African Americans to include their experiences as (more) engaged readers and writers.

In ways similar to *Crisis*'s and *Opportunity*'s outreach, editors of Harlem Renaissance literary anthologies attempted to codify the idea of a New Negro reader more tangibly. After the success of Locke's anthology *The New Negro*, a vibrant market for books about and by African Americans developed. This vibrancy implied a growing African American readership. In response, editors of later anthologies reenvisioned them to further define the artistry that Locke's volume championed and cultivate the practices of a sympathetic and informed reader. As I argue in chapter 3, "Beyond *The New Negro*: Artistry, Audience, and the Harlem Renaissance Literary Anthology," the editors of *Ebony and Topaz, Caroling Dusk,* and *Readings from Negro Authors* framed their volumes, even more than Locke did with *The New Negro*, as mediums of artistic expression. Such editorial practices targeted African American readers, at times secondarily, but affirmed the experience of reading the literary artist and her work.

Through a focus on James Weldon Johnson's use of a developing literary criticism and literary anthologies in his teaching, chapter 4, "Pedagogy for Critical Readership: James Weldon Johnson's English 123," reveals further the pedagogical nature of Harlem Renaissance writers' efforts to impart and to realize their visions of a New Negro reader. For Johnson, this meant transforming young people into critical readers. As I demonstrate, Johnson's lecture notes, bibliography, and course outline provide evidence of his efforts in this regard but also read as complements to Fisk University's mission to have all its students study African American life and culture critically and with affirmation. Given the absence of student responses to English 123, I also read Johnson's references to students' papers and questions as viable indicators of how actual, albeit situated, readers negotiate, and at times redefine, ideas about a New Negro reader that help characterize the Harlem Renaissance.

The New Negro Is Reading

In the Epilogue I underscore the measurable influence that the developing African American reading public had on the publication and reception of the period's literature. I do so to clarify further the extent to which Harlem Renaissance writers' public fashioning of ideal and intended readers is central to the period's legacy. I then reflect on that legacy in an account of my 2013 experience at a joint meeting of two book clubs, Bridging the Chapters and Lovers of Letters, in Sanford, Florida, as their members discussed the novel *Perfect Peace* with its author, Daniel Black.

The approaches to reading that Harlem Renaissance writers modeled in their ideas for a New Negro reader were investments in shaping African Americans, in complex ways, to read, listen, view, and ultimately preserve a range of racially inspired arts. Harlem Renaissance writers' approaches to reading exemplify how African Americans would forge a creative culture in order to practice racial uplift throughout the twentieth century. Richard Wright's seminal 1937 essay "Blueprint for Negro Writing" conveyed this point as well. Although much of the Harlem Renaissance was explicitly concerned with advancing prescriptions for *writing* African American literature, the increased focus on African Americans as a literary audience—as in Wright's own question "Shall Negro writing be for the masses, moulding [sic] the lives and consciousness of those masses toward new goals, or shall it continue begging the question of the Negroes' humanity?"—also produced concurrent public debate about how an African American literature should be read.[45] While subsequent generations of African American creative writers and critics, especially those of the Black Arts movement, would advance Wright's question into a defining motif of their contributions, Harlem Renaissance writers have as part of their legacy the earliest tangible forging of the reciprocal and now historic relationship between African American readers and African American literature.

1

CREATING CRITICAL FRAMEWORKS

Three Models for the New Negro Reader

◆▶◆◀▶

To introduce a new feature of his monthly column "From the Dark Tower," poet and critic Countee Cullen declared to *Opportunity* magazine readers that "what is being read at the Harlem library is a fair index of what books are most in demand by Negroes."[1] With this assertion, Cullen began reporting on the reserve lists for the 135th Street branch, the Harlem branch, of the New York Public Library. The titles making up the first list that Cullen compiled—Theodore Dreiser's *American Tragedy*, Jessie Fauset's *There Is Confusion*, P. C. Wren's *Beau Geste*, Walter White's *Flight*, George Dorsey's *Why We Behave Like Human Beings*, and Alain Locke's *The New Negro*—suggest that patrons of the Harlem branch read broadly and, just like their white contemporaries, targeted both what was popular and what critics deemed worthy.[2] Though published only from December 1926 until July 1927, the reserve list feature furthered public discussion of the value of reading in African America with a necessary focus on what African Americans, in this case patrons of the Harlem branch library, were actually reading. It was in this respect an important step in developing the idea of a New Negro reader, and one that several writers promoted throughout the Harlem Renaissance.

Creating Critical Frameworks

In the January 1927 installment of his column, Cullen signaled a specific interest of Harlem branch patrons when he noted, "We have been having an exciting time of it reading John W. Vandercook's *Tom-Tom*." An account of Vandercook's experiences among the people of Suriname, it was the only book on the branch's reserve lists that Cullen also reviewed in his column. *Tom-Tom*'s draw was, Cullen contended, its "provocation to thought." The book's preface especially "touches us to the quick," he argued, issuing "a protest or two toward our personal interest." Through a collective voice, Cullen interpreted Vandercook's comparative assertion about the development of the United States—" 'Slavery lasted too long and ended too suddenly for the whites to forget and forgive enough to allow the black people into our sancta' "—as "leaving the Negro no share in this gigantic project."[3] In this period of complex juxtapositions of racial pride and patriotism among African Americans, Cullen was attentive to Vandercook's seeming misstep.

The remainder of Cullen's review of *Tom-Tom* anticipated potential responses from *Opportunity*'s black readers who might have questioned why Cullen went on to review a work that so explicitly denied the contributions of African Americans to their own country. Cullen exhibited flexibility, however, in deriving "genuine pleasure" from *Tom-Tom* precisely because Vandercook displayed "thorough sympathy for the inhabitants of Suriname" and gave readers of his work "a picture of persons far more subtle, intelligent, and proud than we have been wont to deem these people whom we have known only by hearsay, not by actual contact on which this author [Vandercook] has based his observations." Here Cullen contrasted approaches to race relations that emerged from bias and stereotype with those that arose from actual interaction. He applauded the latter as the method that produced *Tom-Tom*. According to Cullen, the book's viability also registered through its "language which is an ambush of amuses and covert pricks at both white and colored people in our varying civilization."[4] Cullen qualified his initial objection to *Tom-Tom* with attention to the larger and arguably more important cultural work that it performed, ultimately offering *Opportunity*'s readers a review that engaged in close critical reading aimed at resisting hasty reactions to seemingly disaffirming representations of African Americans. In

CHAPTER 1

isolating *Tom-Tom*'s racial representation, Cullen's review modeled and argued reading practices that were culturally informed and rigorous but flexible. Several writers would name similar characteristics in writing to and through their iterations of a New Negro reader.

In this chapter I illustrate the related but different ways that Harlem Renaissance writers promote and document such reading practices. I specifically consider instances of literary reading that James Weldon Johnson, Jessie Fauset, and Sterling Brown posit throughout the period. Johnson's efforts to establish critical frameworks for engaging African America's arts complemented his influence as a novelist, poet, musician, and NAACP secretary. The thematic range of Johnson's commentary and the venues in which it was published afforded him numerous opportunities to address black and white America as a dual, even rhetorically integrated audience. Similarly, reflecting her training and her own creative work, including the foundational *There Is Confusion,* Jessie Fauset furthered recognition of African America's literary tradition and its potential for critical reading practices. Fauset's efforts made her one of the most influential yet judicious readers of other, usually emergent African American writers. As a seminal folk poet and professor of literature, Sterling Brown tutored the period's reading publics as well, especially as he read and wrote literature to document the artistry in African American life among "the folk." Although he objected to the Harlem Renaissance as a misnomer, Brown displayed equal commitment throughout the period to African American writers and their works and to speaking truthfully to and for African Americans in general.

As influential readers and writers, in their commentary on Harlem Renaissance literature, especially their reviews, these authors often summarized a work, placed it in both literary and historical context, identified its aesthetic qualities, and ultimately articulated to readers whether the work under consideration was worthy of reading or not. Their commentary also defined literature in terms of genre and operated as instances of how to read and assess a contribution to it. Significantly, Johnson's, Fauset's, and Brown's reviews engaged a range of African American readers, from those more experienced with judging literature themselves to those who read literary commentary in newspapers and journals in order to receive and ideally adopt evaluative readings of literary form and its mastery in terms of racial depiction. Their own ways of reading and models for how to read the period's literature, then, projected and called for a New Negro reader attuned to racial representation and able to read for it closely and appropriately, especially the use of dialect and depictions of African America in terms of class.

Among a number of Harlem Renaissance writers, the use of dialect, the linguistic mode of racial representation that Paul Laurence Dunbar famously made into a literary art, was frequently debated as a viable approach. While some commentators staked positions in the middle, the debate persisted largely between those advancing one of two opposing perspectives. There were writers and critics who saw the drive to cultivate African Americans' literary abilities through versifying the speech and depicting the experiences of lower-income and working-class urban or rural American blacks as in some ways as constraining as the racial stereotypes that representations of that speech often provoked. In contrast, others saw the use of dialect or the vernacular in poetry as essential to demonstrating African American artistry, especially African American folk arts. For his part, Johnson read the singular reliance on dialect as limiting, while Fauset recognized its contemporaneous resurgence but saw it as too racially charged, too incompatible with the literary forms that she sought to master. By contrast, Brown employed dialect and argued that it was essential to the production of authentic representations of African American life. As I illustrate in this chapter, the debate that ensued had a particular manifestation in the relationship between Brown and Johnson during the Harlem Renaissance.

Another related idea that informed Johnson's, Fauset's, and Brown's close readings of the period's literature concerned the question of whose experiences best exemplified, if not the fact, then the promise of African American life—its rural and urban masses or its smaller but increasingly influential middle classes. The dynamics of this debate amplified a set of tensions that had earlier been made palpable in the development of postbellum African American literature. As Andreá Williams has noted: "On one hand African Americans who promoted racial uplift questioned whether class antipathies among them might compromise their collective protests for political rights. On the other, African Americans emphasized class differentiation to show that their race could produce representative middle and upper classes distinguished from the uncultured figures who stood for black people in most Americans' imaginations. Both these stances aimed to refute racial prejudice."[5] Echoes of these stances reverberated throughout Harlem Renaissance literature in general and the ways it was read in particular.

For example, Johnson did not value representations of middle-class African American life to the exclusion of those of the folk. Rather, he read any portrayal of African American life as in need of refinement before it could be celebrated as art. Because Fauset viewed depictions of middle-class black life as essential to the work of racial uplift, she conceived of her own novels as counters to entrenched racial stereotypes, which tended to highlight and exploit the experiences of less educated and lower-income rural and urban African Americans. In his creative work and criticism, Brown took issue with the overrepresentation of middle-class experiences and the promotion of so-called refinement; his treatment of Fauset's work in *Negro Caravan* is particularly instructive in this regard. Instead, Brown demonstrated that, meritorious on its own, the real art of and in black life was to be found among the folk. Across a number of venues, the ways of reading that Johnson, Fauset, and Brown practiced and advocated, even when at odds with one another, propelled this literary production as evidence for the assertion that "without great audiences [we cannot] have great literature."[6]

Reading Closely and Comparatively

Johnson's, Fauset's, Brown's, and other Harlem Renaissance writers' orientations toward reading for racial representation offer rich proof of Angelyn Mitchell's later claim that the Harlem Renaissance was "the inaugurating era of African American literary criticism."[7] Forging this inaugural literary criticism established several Harlem Renaissance writers as modern New Negro readers and signal arbiters of how to read (and ultimately write) the works of the period. William Stanley Braithwaite was one such reader of American poetry. As James Smethurst has argued, Braithwaite's work as critic at the *Transcript* and later as editor of many anthologies, especially the annual *Anthology of Magazine Verse* beginning in 1914, allowed Braithwaite to "champion the 'poetry renaissance' " and promote the careers of several writers, including Georgia Douglas Johnson, Robert Frost, Amy Lowell, and Claude McKay.[8] The criticism that Braithwaite and several of his contemporaries fashioned through their reviews grew out of the belief that American literature had achieved a key position in solidifying racial discourse through a host of complex characterizations and depictions.

Because of this history, many Harlem Renaissance writers crafted their poem, novel, or play to convey as much about its genre as about the people and the experiences that the given work's language imaged. This dual focus necessitated engaged, especially close readings of the literature, which writers often modeled on and elicited from their peers as well as from their larger reading public. Indeed, close reading for Harlem Renaissance writers was much more a combination of "attention to words on the page" and to "the context which produced and surrounded them" than was the practice of those typically associated with the proponents of close reading in America at the time. In the case of Johnson, Fauset, and Brown, such close reading amounted to an effort—similar to what Mark Jancovich argued of southern New Critics—to contemplate, critique, and even redress the "condition of culture and society within twentieth-century America."[9] As the record of a critical and culturally aware reader, James Weldon Johnson's *Book of American Negro Poetry*, which I also discuss in subsequent chapters, was an early attempt to counter the notion that African America was not capable of artistry.

Along with the newspapers and journals that influenced them, literary anthologies advanced discussions about African American literature and cultivated readers for it. Beginning as early as 1920, commentary and publication announcements in yearly "reviews of books" suggested that the anthology was gaining status as the Harlem Renaissance's most influential book genre.[10] Whether gathering their letters and reminiscences, political commentary, photographs, or poems, anthologies reflected African Americans' increasing literacy and gestured toward the viability of their social and cultural history. In *The Book of American Negro Poetry*, Johnson noted that his preface had

CHAPTER 1

> gone far beyond what I had in mind when I started. It was my intention to gather the best verses I could find by Negro poets and present them with a bare word of introduction. It was not my plan to make this collection inclusive nor to make the book in any sense a book of criticism. I planned to present only verses by contemporary writers; but, perhaps, because this is the first collection of its kind, I realized the absence of a starting-point and was led to provide one and to fill in with historical data what I felt to be a gap.[11]

Characteristic of a rhetorical style that Johnson often employed in his writing, this aside was more than a direct address to his readers and a deliberate prefatory framing of *The Book of American Negro Poetry*. It also articulated a useful metaphor that conveyed Johnson's understanding of and relationship to his literary audiences.

Indeed, Johnson's literary criticism can well be described as a series of intentional efforts to "fill gaps" between the American reading public that was his focus in the preface and the body of African American literature that his seminal anthology helped celebrate. As he declared to his readers, both black and white, especially those who were unaware of "American Negro poets":

> I make here what may appear to be a more startling statement by saying that the Negro has already proved the possession of [creative] powers by being the creator of the only things artistic that have yet sprung from American soil and been universally acknowledged as distinctive American products. These creations by the American Negro may be summed up under four heads. The first two are the Uncle Remus stories, which were collected by Joel Chandler Harris, and the "spirituals" or slave songs, to which the Fisk Jubilee Singers made the public and the musicians of both the United States and Europe listen. . . . The other two creations are the cakewalk and ragtime. (10)

In describing these "four heads" as creative genres, Johnson not only referenced the increasing appeal of these "distinctive American products" but also framed them for his readers as the confluence of an artistic tradition.

Even if his readers accepted his claim about tradition, Johnson foresaw the potential for lingering questions. One in particular—What made the spiritual or a Cullen poem art?—appears to have influenced how he discussed these genres. His commentary about the "genuine Ragtime song" was instructive in this regard, especially as an important display of the reading practices that united his creative work and social commentary. In quoting "the words of two [songs] that were popular" and through direct address to his readers, Johnson revealed a bit of what had drawn his attention to the song as he read (and listened). After quoting five lines from the song "Po' Boy," Johnson wrote: "These lines are crude, but they contain something of real poetry, of that elusive thing which nobody can define and that you can only tell is there when you feel it. You cannot read these lines without becoming reflective and feeling sorry for 'Po' Boy.' " Johnson urged that lines such as "Mah mammy's lyin' in her grave, / Mah daddy done run away" could and should be *read* as opposed to just being heard. Even more, he suggested that the song had "that elusive thing" that a reader "can only tell is there when [she] feels it" (14–15). Johnson compelled his readers to perceive the song's quality in its ability to foster identification.

The identification that Johnson posited here prefigures the kind of understanding of a reader's engagement with a literary text that Louise Rosenblatt later characterized as the "aesthetic reading." What Johnson described about the process of reading "Po' Boy" is similar to what Rosenblatt referred to as a "reader's moment-to-moment alertness to what is being activated in his consciousness by [a] particular pattern of words during [a] period of actual reading."[12] The "alertness" to one's potential sympathy for Po' Boy was not all that Johnson's close reading of this song documented. He also asserted that reading "Po' Boy" was comparable to the experience of reading poetry. When Johnson noted that the language of "Po' Boy" contained "something of real poetry," he implied that a reader would, and should, recall an experience of reading poetry when reading "Po' Boy." Rather than residing in the form or structure of a referent poem, Johnson suggested, the viability of that referent poem lay in the experience of reading it and in how it made a reader feel. Recalling it would enable a better reading and understanding of "Po' Boy" (arguably representative of similar uses of dialect) not just as a lyric but also in its potential as poetry.

CHAPTER 1

Johnson's attention to the words of "Po' Boy" compelled a consideration of genre that would position a reader to consider the more historically nuanced claim that he articulated in the preface to *The Book of American Negro Poetry*. If a reader's own close reading of "Po' Boy" aided recognition of the raw emotion it expressed and the "crude" language that captured it as (having the potential for) poetry, then Johnson's reader might agree with his assertion that African Americans' music afforded them an almost organic understanding of the literary form (12).

This instance of Johnson's close reading pointedly laid the groundwork for his subsequent efforts to persuade readers of his preface that ragtime and other artistic genres were components and creations of "Negro Genius." In this way Johnson framed his anthology through a strategy of reading dialect for both its effect and its artistry, especially its poetic viability. Later in the preface, Johnson further developed his reading of artistry through attention to Phillis Wheatley's poetry. Johnson's consideration of Wheatley's artistry advanced and implicitly modeled comparative analysis as an instructive strategy for reading the artistry of racial representation.

Turning to Wheatley's work, Johnson contended that "the American Negro has accomplished something in pure literature," adding that "the list of those who have done so would be surprising both by its length and the excellence of the achievements" (22). "Such a list," he argued, "begins with Phillis Wheatley." Johnson contextualized her primacy to "fill another gap" for his reader: "It seems strange that the books [on literature] generally give space to a mention of Urian Oakes, President of Harvard College, and to quotations from the crude and lengthy elegy which he published in 1667; and print examples from the execrable versified version of the Psalms made by New England divines, and yet deny a place to Phillis Wheatley" (23). Rather than explore the strangeness that might explain this historical exclusion, Johnson invited his readers to join him in correcting this aspect of American and African American literary history. The opportunity he offered to read Wheatley's and Anne Bradstreet's poetry comparatively as "first in order of time of all the women poets in America" extended that invitation (23).

Johnson urged readers to contrast Wheatley's "Imagination" with Brad-

Creating Critical Frameworks

street's earlier "Contemplation" and "take them both at their best and in the same vein"(24). Other than asserting, "We do not think that the black woman suffers much by comparison with the white," Johnson made no comment about what captured his attention in the lines he excerpted (24). This was work that he left to his readers. He encouraged that comparative work, however, by reminding readers that Bradstreet "was wealthy, [a] cultivated Puritan girl," while Wheatley "was a Negro slave girl born in Africa" (24). With a subsequent note that Wheatley had been "kept out of most of the books[,] especially text-books on literature [then] used in schools," Johnson prompted readers to employ close reading and comparative analysis to consider whether Wheatley's poem revealed parity with Bradstreet's (23). By advocating such reading methods in his preface, Johnson suggested to readers that American literary history was shaped by a complex field of racial representation. In doing so he also equipped readers with an approach for considering the poems that followed.

Johnson's volume was not a generic literary history. First and foremost, it was a collection that celebrated the words and images of African America as poetry and art. Even with Wheatley's focus on religion, addresses to prominent white male figures, and use of poetic forms circulating at a time when "Pope and Gray were supreme," Johnson positioned her as a progenitor to a literary tradition that cultivated "race consciousness" into art (25, 28). His survey of the "four times in single lines [when Wheatley] refer[ed] to herself as 'Afric's muse' " provided another opportunity for Johnson's reader to engage with literature, Wheatley's poetry in this case, as the art of and a repository for racial representation (28). After quoting the lines "Ye blooming plants of human race divine, / An Ethiop tells you 'tis your greatest foe," Johnson followed with the observation that "one looks in vain for some outburst or even complaint against the bondage of her people, for some agonizing cry about her native land" (28). Johnson's lament here was more a commentary about a particular thematic absence than it was an evaluation of Wheatley's artistry overall. Notwithstanding, in wondering what Wheatley's poetry would yield if she had emphasized *that* racial theme, Johnson signaled such an expectation as a reasonable reaction from an engaged reader of early African American poetry.

To read for racial representation with such expectation and then determine whether or not the poet who offered such emphasis had also produced art required more than noting a mere reference to or explicit use of a racial theme. The attention to artistry that Johnson modeled for his readers was ultimately meant to inspire consideration of how a black poet saw "objectively" African America's "humor, its superstitions, its shortcomings," felt "sympathetically its heart-wounds, its yearnings, its aspirations, and . . . voice[d] them all in a purely literary form" (34–35). Since, according to Johnson, neither Wheatley nor her immediate literary descendants "strike a deep native strain," he urged reading African American poets' racial themes based on the work of later poets, including George Horton and Frances Harper (34). In Johnson's estimation, Paul Laurence Dunbar was the exemplar, and the structural primacy of Dunbar's poems in *The Book of American Negro Poetry*, nine of which open the volume, reinforced Johnson's claim.

Reading for Artistry in the Mastery of Form

As an anthology, *The Book of American Negro Poetry* was an important, even ambitious effort to shape the period's literature and literary criticism. Responses from his peers provided a useful gauge of its and Johnson's impact during the Harlem Renaissance. For example, in her review column "As to Books," Jessie Fauset assured *Crisis* readers in 1922 that *The Book of American Negro Poetry* "has the value of an arrow pointing in the direction of Negro genius, but the author's preface has a more immediate worth. It is not only a graceful piece of expository writing befitting a collection of poetry, but it affords a splendid compendium of the Negro's artistic contributions to America."[13] If Fauset's review displayed a command of the evidence that Johnson presented to argue for "Negro genius," it also affirmed Johnson's project of anthologizing poetry to reflect African American artistry. Fauset's comments thus furthered the idea of a New Negro reader as "neither an abstraction nor an actual living reader, but a hybrid—a real reader . . . who does everything within [her] power to make [herself] informed."[14] While influential anthologies such as *The Book of American Negro Poetry* courted the type of informed reader that Fauset was, they were neither the only nor even the primary ways in which Harlem Renaissance readers engaged such displays of African American artistry. The literary tradition that Johnson argued for progressed, albeit in abbreviated form, through the weekly and monthly African American press. This network of newspapers and journals also served as important venues for advancing public discussions about how to read and thereby identify the merits of the poetry, fiction, and drama published as part of the Harlem Renaissance.

Coverage of the galvanizing New York Urban League and Writers' Guild celebration of Fauset's first novel, *There Is Confusion,* in March 1924 illustrated well how the African American press read and compelled readings of these merits as an instance of racial uplift. In particular, fellow poet and journalist Georgia Douglas Johnson's story for the *Pittsburgh Courier* headlined "Race Authors in Dinner to Praise Jessie Fauset for New Novel on Negro" underscored as exemplary the fact that "literary New York has responded warmly, enthusiastically and most sympathetically to the call of the young writers' guild." In Douglas Johnson's estimation, "express[ing] appreciation for [Fauset's] literary effort" was as important as "mark[ing] a beginning in cooperative literary and [sic] endeavor."[15] Through articles such as Douglas Johnson's, the African American press not only envisioned audiences as interracial in composition but also chronicled this event as the type of news in which African American readers were interested. In holding up all of "literary New York" as an exemplar, Douglas Johnson's report on the debut of Fauset's novel appealed, in one direction, to readers who took note of racial firsts and valued literature as an exhibition of African Americans' social progress. In another, related direction, Douglas Johnson subtly tutored the inexperienced among those readers and encouraged them to take part in such celebrations while responding to them as opportunities to read such instances of African American artistry.

As literary editor of the NAACP's *Crisis,* Fauset similarly ensured visibility for African American writers and encouraged other African Americans, who constituted nearly 80 percent of the journal's readership, to read these writers' works.[16] Just as the ability to master the form of a given literary genre was a quality that Fauset aspired to as a novelist and poet, she in turn read for this quality in the works of her predecessors and contemporaries. She argued that such artistry would best construct an African American literary tradition and render it comparable to the most venerated of the world's literary traditions.

Such was the case with her 1926 reviews of Countee Cullen's *Color* and Langston Hughes's collection *The Weary Blues*. In her review of *Color*, for example, Fauset attended to Cullen's characteristic and adept use of the sonnet and other gestures toward English poetry but also read the strength of his artistry in poems that "[arose] out of the consciousness of being a 'Negro in a day like this' in America."[17] Fauset listed representative titles from *Color*, which included "Yet Do I Marvel," "Heritage," and "The Pagan Prayer," to direct her reader's attention to signal works, especially his use of sonnets, which were, as Michael Bibby has argued, "often cited as a sign of black modernization and cultural advancement."[18] She then provided some evidence for her claim that "to pour forth poignantly and sincerely the innerness of life which black men live calls for special understanding."[19]

With an excerpt from Cullen's "Heritage," Fauset suggested that a poet's ability to render experience through the stanza, what she described as "four illuminating lines," was a viable measure of artistry. With these representative lines, Fauset argued, Cullen "[unpacked] . . . the psychology of colored Americans, that strange extra dimension which totally artificial conditions have forced into sharp reality." Here, Fauset suggested, Cullen echoed the period's language of racial pride but recast its mood through the lines of his poetry that she isolated, specifically "All day long and all night through / One thing only I must do: / Quench my pride and cool my blood, / Lest I perish in the flood." In "Heritage," Fauset contended, Cullen offered "a new expression of a struggle now centuries old," declaring, "Here I am convinced is Mr. Cullen's forte; he has the feeling and the gift to express colored-ness in a world of whiteness" (238).

Unlike Johnson's treatment of "Po' Boy," Fauset's review of *Color* lacked an explicit focus on the reader's experience. Instead, it documented her close reading of Cullen's word choice for the tone it conveyed and the imagery it produced. In this way, Fauset encouraged *Crisis*'s readers not only to seek out Cullen's volume but also, in reading it, to consider

Cullen's poetry as an important articulation of New Negro consciousness through renowned forms. Although there were ideological differences, the major Harlem Renaissance periodicals were similar in reinforcing African Americans' collective sensibility as agents within and of a racially affirming and literate public culture. This was especially true in *Crisis*. As Anne Carroll has demonstrated, W. E. B. Du Bois's editorship during this period was largely responsible for *Crisis*'s pioneering "coverage of its two most prominent topics: protest against racial injustice and affirmation of the achievements of African Americans."[20] With regular departments such as "The Horizon" and "The Looking Glass," NAACP branch updates, and Fauset's review columns, *The Crisis* functioned as a vehicle for one's advancement—as a human being, a citizen, and an informed reader.

Lauded as Cullen's *Color* was, the artistry it exhibited did not become the standard. As much a consequence of their concurrent debuts as of Fauset's commitment to showing *Crisis* readers (and the world) the diversity within African America's artistry that she found appropriate, Fauset followed her review of *Color* with one of Hughes's first volume, *The Weary Blues*, documenting her engaged reading of it. Fauset opened the review by recounting her "first literary acquaintance" with Hughes. Her "very perfect . . . memory" of the occasion conveyed her affection for Hughes and provided another instance of the ways in which Fauset mentored the Harlem Renaissance's younger generation of writers (239). She reviewed Hughes's poetry through a framework similar to the one she employed in her treatment of Cullen's poems. While she read for the artistry of his racial representations, she also recognized his versatility and his ability to move between venerated forms and employ a diversity of themes.

Her reading of an excerpt from Hughes's "Song for a Banjo Dance" is an example. Referring to lines from the poem's first and second stanzas, especially "Shake your brown feet, honey" and "The sun's going down this very night / Might never rise no mo," Fauset argued: "Now this is very significant, combining as it does the doctrine of the Old Biblical exhortation, 'eat, drink, and be merry for tomorrow ye die,' Horace's 'Carpe diem,' the German 'Freut euch des Lebens' and Herrick's 'Gather ye rosebuds while ye may.' This is indeed a universal subject served Negro-style and though I am no great lover of dialect I hope heartily that Mr. Hughes will give us many more such combinations" (238). To advance her contention here, Fauset excerpted the poem for her *Crisis* readers and then interpreted its lines as part of a tradition of literary allusions about the precariousness of life. Whether or not Hughes actually composed his lines with such referents in mind, Fauset's assertion compelled readers to consider his ability to render universal themes through an African American perspective. Her qualified invitation for him to produce more "combinations" of this type underscored the artistry of his depiction and reinforced the idea that it was a quality for which a New Negro reader should read.

Notwithstanding her call for more treatments of universal themes, the central premise of Fauset's review of *The Weary Blues* had to do with the way Hughes wrote to and from African American experiences. Fauset addressed her reader in a tone that was appreciative of Hughes yet persuasive, writing of Hughes: "While I do not think of him as a protagonist of color,—he is too much the citizen of the world for that—, I doubt if any one will ever write more tenderly, more understandingly, more humorously of the life of Harlem shot through as it is with mirth, abandon and pain. Hughes comprehends this life, has studied it and loved it" (239). As representative proof, Fauset concluded her review of *The Weary Blues* with an excerpt from the poem "Cabaret," saying that it demonstrated how Hughes's poetry "epitomized [Harlem's] essence":

> Does a jazz-band ever sob?
> They say a jazz-band's gay.
> Yet as the vulgar dancers whirled
> And the wan night wore away,
> One said she heard the jazz-band sob
> When the little dawn was grey. (239)

Here, again, Fauset drew *Crisis* readers' attention to tone and imagery. Although she did not elaborate on how the poem "epitomized" Harlem, the suggestion of jazz musicians' complex humanity in the poem, what Kevin Young reads as the way Hughes "took tragedy and made it heroic, finding it comic too," was likely evidence for the association on which Fauset remarked.[21]

Creating Critical Frameworks

Attention to the form of "Cabaret" was not referenced in Fauset's reading of Hughes's ability to represent the core of Harlem. While she did appreciate the modern quality of his representations of African America, Fauset encouraged his mastery of forms beyond the blues and jazz aesthetic he often employed.[22] Nevertheless, as James Smethurst has argued, Hughes's use of the blues especially led to a compelling innovation of form as he "broke the lines in two at the caesura so that this typical blues poetry stanza was six lines instead of three," an adaptation that "became the standard for blues verse in American poetry throughout the twentieth century."[23] Fauset's commentary about Hughes's dexterity and Cullen's mastery of form advanced her reviews beyond celebratory announcements. Such focus reflected a critical discourse regarding racial representation that many of the period's advocates deemed necessary for a viable literature. Fauset made this advocacy particularly explicit in one of the Harlem Renaissance's most pointed debates about the writing and reading of African American literature.

In her contributions to *Crisis*'s famed 1926 symposium "The Negro in Art: How Shall He Be Portrayed," Fauset's pointed answers conveyed an understanding of the comparative racial and national implications of African Americans' literary production that Johnson frequently targeted and also stressed a set of attitudes, even passions, that were necessary to produce quality writing. Her answer to the questionnaire's fourth query—"What are Negroes to do when they are continually painted at their worst and judged by the public as they are painted?"—is worth printing in its entirety: "They must protest strongly to get their protestations before the public. But more than that they must learn to write with a humor, a pathos, a sincerity so evident and a delineation so fine and distinctive that their portraits, even of the 'best Negroes,' those presumably most like 'white folks,' will be acceptable to publisher and reader alike."[24] Fauset identified the intersection of market and ideological forces that drove this debate. Her reference to "publisher and reader" suggested that possessing such attitudes was only part of the formula for redress; for Fauset, Harlem Renaissance writers had to embrace and fuse such attitudes into recognizable forms. Loosely veiled rejoinders to criticisms of her own work, Fauset's use of quotation marks emphasized her comments about race and class. The device advanced her insistence that regardless of what subjects a writer chose to represent literarily, such depiction should be deployed through a resonant and accepted form. For Fauset, this was the true measure of an African American writer's artistry and, therefore, the primary quality that a New Negro reader should consider.

Reading as Critical Reflection

Sterling Brown's 1931 essay "Our Literary Audience" is an instructive, complementary example of how the Harlem Renaissance's literary criticism depended on the instances of engaged, close readings that Johnson, Fauset, and other writers offered and that reflected, to borrow from Katherine Capshaw Smith, "the impetus to validate versions of black identity in print."[25] Brown's critique of the period's reading publics punctuated the increase in the number and diversity of perspectives on African Americans' literature that had emerged in the almost ten years since Johnson's *Book of American Negro Poetry*. Instead of a line from a lyric or stanza from a poem, Brown excerpted public opinion and employed close reading to address and engage his readers in a critical exchange about the way other African Americans influenced what it meant to read their literature. What Brown related about African Americans as an audience reads as painstaking commentary on the logic and influence of intra-group perspectives. Unlike the more interracial accounts that filled the African American press, Brown's "Our Literary Audience" focused on African Americans' unrealized potential as readers.

Brown was one of several columnists to forge public discussion of literature as a critical facet of black civil society. In particular, following Charles Johnson's departure as *Opportunity*'s editor in the early 1930s, Brown and Alain Locke continued the work of reviewing African American literature for the journal. Brown's column "The Literary Scene: Chronicle and Comment" was one of the most consistent exhibitions of the authority that Harlem Renaissance writers had achieved in shaping the direction and content of the period's racial discourse. His column ran virtually monthly from December 1930 to December 1935, and throughout this period Brown wrote with fervor and an intimacy that reflected the long-standing practice in the

African American press of addressing readers directly. A writer in real possession of the attitudes that Fauset called for in *Crisis*'s "Negro in Art" symposium, Brown especially exhibited this fervor and intimacy through "Our Literary Audience," written in addition to his regular *Opportunity* column. One of the related and enduring features of both his column and his essay is Brown's use of the first-person plural. It expressed Brown's familiarity with the literature he discussed as much as it acknowledged *Opportunity*'s African American readers as his intended audience. With that now familiar consideration of the black writer's curious position, Brown delivered an assessment of a reading public that received little explicit attention.

Employing what might be called a social science discourse, Brown chose to present a list of general behaviors rather than a literary excerpt as his first instance of close reading. "Our criticism," he informed his readers, contained "certain fallacies" which he had "detect[ed] within at least the last six years."[26] In the preceding decade, much discussion had circulated about the worth of that criticism and the African American literature on which it reflected, including anthologies such as Locke's *The New Negro*, a spate of literary contests, and first publications such as Georgia Douglas Johnson's *The Heart of a Woman*, Claude McKay's *Harlem Shadows*, and Walter White's *The Fire in the Flint*.[27] There had also been a resurgence of literary clubs throughout African America. Taken together, these and other literary developments provided Brown much to draw on in describing these four related "fallacies":

> We look upon Negro books regardless of the author's intention, as representative of all Negroes, i.e., as sociological documents.
>
> We insist that Negro books must be idealistic, optimistic tracts for race advertisement.
>
> We are afraid of truth telling, of satire.
>
> We criticize from the point of view of bourgeois America, of racial apologists.[28]

Brown's own experiences reading and writing from within African America helped him articulate how these "certain fallacies" revealed the limitations of racial uplift. Here, Brown recognized a middle-class consciousness (actual and aspiring) and drew attention to the racial illogic that some African Americans employed when they read works about and by other African Americans. It was an illogic that Brown made visible and that he intended through his own critical reading to correct.

Brown developed his analysis through examples of "supersensitive criticism" that his representative "we" produced in a notable moment of literary and artistic production through a replay of reactions to one of Eugene O'Neill's landmark dramas. Brown followed an instance of racial illogic surrounding the controversial yet popular play *The Emperor Jones* to its likely conclusion, reasoning that if his "we" argued emphatically that O'Neill was " 'showing us the Negro race,' not a shrewd Pullman Porter [in protagonist Brutus Jones], who had for a space, a run of luck," then "by the same token, is Smithers [the drama's white antagonist] a picture of the white race? If so, O'Neill is definitely propagandizing against the Caucasian. O'Neill must be an East Indian" (43). Here Brown mirrored back reactions that he deemed representative of selective and limiting misreading among a growing segment of African American readers and then crafted the very satire that he argued this particular audience did not recognize as literary or artistic. Through a keen awareness of the deleterious effects of racial stereotypes and misrepresentation, Brown explained well the real reactions that he exaggerated. Recalling to some extent Cullen's earlier exhortations, what Brown wanted from African American readers was a greater degree of sophisticated and balanced interpretation. African Americans' development of literature in the face of a persistent and pervasive racial prejudice, he argued, meant that "when [racial prejudice] raises its head, it is up to us to strike, and strike hard. But when it doesn't exist, there is no need of tilting at windmills" (43).

Brown addressed readers from his perspective as an artist to consolidate the engaged close reading that was "Our Literary Audience" into a persuasive redefinition of racial representation as a measure of literary merit. He concluded his article by making the point that "Negro artists have enough to contend with in getting a hearing, in isolation, in the peculiar problems that beset all artists, in the mastery of form and in the understanding of life. It would be no less disastrous to demand of them that they shall evade truth, that they shall present us a Pollyanna philosophy of life, that, to suit our prejudices, they shall lie. It would mean that as self-respecting artists they could no longer exist" (61). Here was another of Brown's rhetorical moves aimed at connecting with yet changing the perspective of his black readers. Because "self-respect" mattered, Brown asserted in the uncritical appeals for truth that he critiqued, the collective we, specific to members of a black middle class and representative of the mass of African Americans that it implicated, should have appreciated his reasoning.

While affirming a writer's choice to see and reproduce art in her experience, Brown's assertions effected more than a rationale for artistic autonomy. He offered a collaborative model, one that turned on engaged self-reflexive close readings by both black writers and other black readers. While not an exploration of the ethical dimensions of reading that J. Hillis Miller or Wayne Booth undertook in the latter part of the twentieth century, Brown's contentions were invested in fostering informed reading practices and forging criticism that included "aesthetic formalism" as well as recognition of "literature's power over how we live our lives."[29] Ultimately, Brown looked beyond the literary text to point to the way African Americans read and discussed the period's literature as an important site of racial representation. His consideration of such "criticism" projected a New Negro reader thoughtfully aware that what she brought to a text paired in important ways with what she took from it. "Our Literary Audience" advocated a shared responsibility for racial representation in the acts of literary reading that African Americans undertook.

The literary culture that Brown envisioned in "Our Literary Audience" had significant implications for the approaches to and practices of reading that writers advanced throughout the Harlem Renaissance. More willing to see, study, and celebrate the complexities in African America's diversity through dialect and in the experiences of African American laborers and rural folk, to name a few, Brown critiqued and qualified positions that, for example, Johnson and Fauset maintained. For Brown, they marginalized and even excluded depictions about black folk. Given the infamous tensions among Harlem Renaissance writers such as those between the "generations" of writers producing and promoting the period's literature, perspectives on what one should read for when one read as a New Negro reflected, as Lawrence Hogue has noted, "the various literary and ideological forces that actually cause certain texts to be published, promoted, and certified and others to be subordinated and/or excluded."[30] Indeed, such forces informed Brown's close readings of Johnson's and Fauset's works during the period.

Brown acknowledged the need to forge a literary tradition through attention to its artists. Years after Johnson's death in 1938, Brown penned a related reflection on Johnson's work in *Negro Caravan*. "By his interpretations of Negro poetry and music, by occasional essays on the problems of Negro writers, and by his own creative work," Brown argued, "Johnson succeeded more than any predecessor in furthering the cause of the Negro artist."[31] Notwithstanding the reverence that he displayed for Johnson here, Brown also employed his close readings to counter critical reactions to African American writers' increased use of dialect during the Harlem Renaissance, especially Johnson's disagreement with the idea that dialect should serve as a primary source of African America's artistry.

The first public salvo in the debates between Brown and Johnson over dialect came in the preface to *The Book of American Negro Poetry*. In it, Johnson argued the need for an African American poet akin to Ireland's John Millington Synge, contending that such a poet "needs a form that is freer and larger than dialect, but which will still hold the racial flavor; a form expressing the imagery, the idioms, the peculiar turns of thought and the distinctive humor and pathos, too, of the Negro, but which will also be capable of voicing the deepest and highest emotions and aspirations, and allow [for] the widest range of subjects and the widest scope of treatment." As he asserted later in the preface, Johnson's critique was "no [precarious] indictment against dialect as dialect but [rather] against the mold of convention in which Negro dialect in the United States has been set." He called for a day when "the colored poet in the United States [would] sit down to write in dialect without feeling that his first line [would] put the reader in a frame of mind which demands that the poem be humorous or pathetic."[32]

Given his own use of dialect and African American folk life as subjects of his poetry, Brown had no reason to mask his sympathies. For him, lines such as "Death, ain't yuh got no shame?" and "Life for me ain't been no crystal stair" refuted such expectations. They offered as well voices of authentic experience, not retrogressive signs of constrained artistry. Brown addressed Johnson directly in "Our Literary Audience," arguing, for example, "Mr. Johnson is responsible for a very acute criticism of dialect," then adding: "There is nothing 'degraded' about dialect. Dialectical peculiarities are universal. There is something about Negro dialect, in the idiom, the turn of phrase, the music of the vowels and consonants that is worth treasuring."[33] Brown believed that modernity still had a place for the poetry in African Americans' dialect. His rebuttal—an instance of the engaged reading that he advocated across his writings—alerted other African American readers to the artistry in this linguistic mode as well.

As one of Brown's intended and actual readers, Johnson understood Brown's arguments—as his reading of "Po' Boy," cited earlier, demonstrates—but remained convinced that dialect was a cultural resource from which to depart, not one for the African American poet to explore indefinitely. Johnson even celebrated Brown's poetry as exemplary in this regard. When Brown's first book of poems, *Southern Road*, was published in 1932, Johnson wrote the introduction and praised Brown for having in effect discovered how to write a black vernacular poetry that was not burdened by the expectation for only "dialect verse" that Paul Laurence Dunbar had encountered thirty years earlier. Brown "has made more than mere transcriptions of folk poetry," Johnson wrote, "and he has done more than bring to it mere artistry; he has deepened its meanings and multiplied its implications."[34] Johnson also showed his respect for Brown by inviting him to write the *Outline for the Study of the Poetry of American Negroes*, a teacher's guide to accompany Johnson's anthology.[35] Not surprisingly, when discussing Johnson's own poetry in the *Outline*, Brown situated Johnson—just as he did Dunbar, their revered predecessor—as a poet who understood the artistry of African American folk expression, specifically dialect, and then employed extracts from Johnson's own work to validate the vernacular as essential to critical, especially academic, study of African American poetry.

In a description of Johnson's "Listen, Lord," for example, Brown directed readers of the *Outline* to "notice how for this poem too the poet has gone back to the folk material."[36] What he advocated for in close readings of Johnson's poetry, Brown directed Harlem Renaissance readers to consider more generally when they read the works of other writers. In his 1937 *Nation* review of Zora Neale Hurston's *Their Eyes Were Watching God*, Brown treated Janie, Hurston's protagonist, as though she were a real person rather than a character in a novel. He opened the review with the words "Janie's grandmother, remembering how in slavery she was used 'for a work-ox and a brood sow,'" then included an excerpt from *Their Eyes* to underscore his description of Hurston's novel as "chock-full of earthy and touching poetry," for instance, "Ah don't want yo' feathers always crumpled by folks throwin' up things in yo' face."[37] Brown demonstrated both the authenticity of Janie's experiences and Hurston's ability to verify it through Janie's representative folk speech. He also praised Hurston for advancing the African American novel while celebrating the fictional residents of Eatonville as having the "unabashed shrewdness of the Blues" when contemplating "human needs and frailties."[38]

The influence of Brown's impassioned refusal to "accept formula approaches to black literature and stereotyped responses to black people" is not simply manifested in how he countered misreadings of dialect in Harlem Renaissance literature and celebrated its artistry.[39] It was also clear in his responses to depictions of middle-class black life as the preferred and expected way to portray African America. Brown completed many reviews that encouraged depictions of the folk or that critiqued their absence and incorporated similar close readings in furthering an African American literary tradition. His 1937 volume *The Negro in American Fiction* is an instructive example. Described by Alain Locke as differing from the "usual academic survey[s]" in giving "a penetrating analysis of the social factors and attitudes behind the various schools and periods considered," *The Negro in American Fiction* organized African American fiction historically but also made the point that the genre was predominant in and even essential to any study of African American letters as a literary tradition.[40] Brown's mission to showcase the artistry in African American folk life recurs throughout the volume but often as a complement to his notions about, among other things, class, stereotypes, the influence of white authors, and, as he argued, the "responsibility [on the part of African American novelists] of being the ultimate portrayers of their own" (4).

It was with Fauset's depictions of class that Brown took issue in a close reading of her works. After situating Fauset's four novels—*There Is Confusion, Plum Bun, The Chinaberry Tree,* and *Comedy, American Style*—as a subgenre of the "Urban Scene" which he referred to as "Bourgeois Realism," Brown aligned Fauset's novels with a range of other works, including Gertrude Sanborn's *Veiled Aristocrats,* Nella Larsen's *Quicksand,* Geoffrey Barnes's *Dark Lustre,* and Fannie Hurst's *Imitation of Life,* noting: "Continuing the earlier apologist tradition, with propaganda a little less direct, certain novelists have set out to prove the presence of a Negro upper-class, and to deplore the injustices of its lot. Their standards are bourgeois; they respect characters in ratio to their color, breeding, gentility, wealth and prestige. 'Realism' is perhaps a misnomer, if these novels are judged by their plots, which are seldom very life-like; the realism is chiefly in the settings" (139).[41] He accepted Fauset's choice to write about "the class of Negroes [that] she knows." If he questioned the authenticity of her novels, it was not because they lacked any treatment of the folk but rather because "instead of more typical Negro middle class experience we get [in Fauset's novels] the more spectacular 'passing' and exceptional Negro artists and cosmopolitans" (142).

Apparently Brown and Fauset did not debate their differing perspectives in the ways that Brown and Johnson did. Nevertheless, her earlier comments in *Crisis* justifying an African American writer's (and by implication her own) choice to depict middle-class black life and Brown's assessments of the same in *The Negro in American Fiction* indirectly constituted, if not a continuum of approaches, then palpably opposed positions on how to read and write the literary depictions of African American life that Harlem Renaissance readers encountered. Brown did not simply dispute the purportedly representative nature of Fauset's novels, however. He gave close readings of her own words, those of her characters, and other readers in order to do so. His rejoinder to what Joanne Gabbin later described as William Stanley Braithwaite's "overestimation" of the value of Fauset's novel's is instructive in this regard.[42]

What Brown objected to was Braithwaite's contention that Fauset was the "American woman most worthy to 'wear the mantle of Jane Austen's genius' " (141–42). Attempting to disrupt the canonizing potential of Braithwaite's assessment, he argued, "This comparison is not apt: Jane Austen's satiric approach to her people and setting and her neatly logical plots are not evident in Miss Fauset's four novels," concluding: "Miss Fauset is sentimental, and regardless of her disclaimers, is an apologist. She records a class in order to praise a race" (142). Brown's counterargument and close readings worked together to effect a dismissal of Fauset's contributions—the type of marginalization that, as several scholars have noted, Fauset clearly understood and abhorred from its first manifestation at the celebrated 1924 Civil Club dinner that the National Urban League's *Opportunity* sponsored through later assessments such as Brown's and countered in subsequent rereadings of Fauset's work.[43]

Whether through speeches, essays, and articles, hosting literary gatherings, or their own literary productions, however, several women writers voiced agendas for changing the economic, social, and political realities facing African Americans in general and women in particular. Fauset was one among several of the Harlem Renaissance's women writers to convey and depict the complexities of black women's experiences, oftentimes as explicit responses to the production of demeaning and stereotypical images of black women.[44] Take, for example, the struggle of a black female youth as depicted in Gwendolyn Bennett's "To a Dark Girl"; the depiction of how racism affects a middle-class black woman's life choices in Angelina Grimké's *Rachel;* the folk experiences of character Delia Jones in Zora Neale Hurston's "Sweat"; or the intersections of class and color in the life of Nella Larsen's Helga Crane in *Quicksand*.[45] Were it not for Fauset's own, highly visible readings of literature, comparatively prolific depictions of African American life, and the affirming, engaged close readings of her work from several of her peers throughout the period, the racism and sexism circumscribing African American women's lives, specifically their public discourse, might have rendered a record of African American literacy and literary practices even more a male phenomenon than it has been historically.

◆▸·◂◆

Creating Critical Frameworks

Although Sterling Brown published more engaged close readings of African American literature than did James Weldon Johnson and Jessie Fauset, he mostly championed one way to read and write African American life. Brown's insistence on depictions of the folk as necessary for displaying the truth of those experiences contrasted with Johnson's general refining aims and Fauset's more specific middle-class depictions. That all three writers read literature through these representative orientations, and did so publicly, reveals the deepening nature of the literature and its criticism as a tradition. Evidenced in how they reviewed Harlem Renaissance literature, at times one another's works, these differing perspectives and a shared commitment to the production of literature of high quality shaped Johnson's, Fauset's, and Brown's public (and, to a degree, private) relationships but also positioned them as New Negro readers. This creative conflict also informed how they similarly exhibited their close readings as models for other African American readers to follow. In their different but related approaches to representing African America literarily were visions of and explicit calls for a New Negro readership.

For Johnson, Fauset, and Brown, that readership would develop an appreciation for the period's literature predicated on historical knowledge and continuous close reading. It would welcome the artistry of racial representation. It would balance, if not suspend, its racialized expectations and projections in recognition of the need for and in support of artistic autonomy. Writing about and to these implications of African American readership through the journals and anthologies of the Harlem Renaissance, Johnson, Fauset, and Brown hoped to further the production of and garner engaged readership for what many celebrated as a rich and transformative literature.

IN SEARCH OF BLACK WRITERS (AND READERS)
Crisis's *and* Opportunity's *Literary Contests*

◆▶✦◀◆

A literary contest—one that paid aspiring writers for and then published their submissions—may not immediately reveal the idea of a New Negro reader that persisted throughout the Harlem Renaissance. But the famed awards that the NAACP's publication *The Crisis,* under W. E. B. Du Bois, and the National Urban League's *Opportunity* sponsored in the mid-1920s were public exhibitions of what it meant to read the literature that writers such as Jessie Fauset, Walter White, Langston Hughes, and Zora Neale Hurston produced during the period. As two of the era's most influential journals, *Crisis* and *Opportunity* not only helped fashion African Americans into a national reading public, especially for the poetry, fiction, and drama penned by young writers, but also served as important mediums for modeling how to read and write as a New Negro. With these literary contests, specifically the announcements and editorials publicizing the prizes, criteria for submission, and judges' comments, *Crisis* and *Opportunity* appealed to readers as emergent writers and influenced how submissions were crafted as much as how those texts were to be read. These contests encouraged the alignment of accepted standards of craft with somewhat more malleable conventions of racial representation. They also courted and then documented African American creativity as an element of America's modernity.

Among the dynamics that evidence the Harlem Renaissance as a social movement, *Crisis*'s and *Opportunity*'s literary contests galvanized the emphasis of the African American press and racial uplift organizations on literacy and literature as tools for social change. When it came to inspiring racial pride among these journals' African American readership as part of that emphasis, their literary contests exemplified what Nathan Huggins would later call the "vogue of the New Negro." For Huggins, it "had all of the character of a public relations promotion. The Negro had to be 'sold' to the public in terms they could understand. Not the least important target in this campaign was the Negro himself; he had to be convinced of his worth. It is important to understand this, because much of the art and letters that was the substance on which the New Negro was built and which made up the so-called Harlem Renaissance was serving this promotional end."[1] As Huggins suggested, simply to assert that some African Americans had become noteworthy writers would not shift the negative perceptions of African Americans more generally and related dynamics circumscribing black life. To produce such a shift in race relations required, among other factors, a flood of creative output. Additionally, in order to achieve such output among African Americans, *Crisis*, *Opportunity*, and other such publications would have to (and did) target black readers specifically and sustain their outreach to them.

Crisis's and *Opportunity*'s literary contests and their range of sponsors consolidated the promotion of a New Negro reader undertaken by both journals throughout the period. They were efforts at racial advancement that sought to foster good literature which represented African America in a positive light. *Opportunity* editor Charles S. Johnson's rationale for his journal's venture into this particular mode of promotion conveyed this point:

> The purpose, then, of *Opportunity*'s literary contest can be thus stated in brief: It hopes to stimulate and encourage creative literary effort among Negroes; to locate and orient Negro writers of ability; to stimulate and encourage interest in the serious development of

CHAPTER 2

> a body of literature about Negro life, drawing deeply upon these tremendously rich resources; to encourage the reading of literature both by Negro authors and about Negro life, not merely because they are Negro authors but because what they write is literature and because the literature is interesting; to foster a market for Negro writers and for literature by and about Negroes; to bring these writers into contact with the general world of letters to which they have been for the most part timid and inarticulate strangers; to stimulate and foster a type of writing by Negroes which shakes itself free of deliberate propaganda and protest.[2]

Johnson's statement of multiple purposes for *Opportunity*'s contests appeared in the journal's September 1924 issue and echoed a growing sentiment shared by several of his contemporaries about the potential and viability of African American letters at the time. Just as *Opportunity* would do throughout its period of publication, the African American press in general both encouraged and documented this feeling. Some white observers, including patrons, publishers, and critics as well as the lay reading public, contributed to the interracial reach of this effort.

Equally important for Johnson, African Americans came to identify, beyond newspapers and journals, with the prospect of a "serious development of a body of literature about Negro life" at schools, local libraries, churches, and book clubs. Reflecting this dynamic, Johnson's announcement, more a decisive "call for writers," conveyed the idea that the contests made more tangible the opportunity to represent African Americans' advancement and sought to find and train the best poets, novelists, playwrights, and essayists within African America to foster this collective sensibility. The social context that Johnson referred to in his announcement underlined the role of *Crisis*'s and *Opportunity*'s literary contests as facets of American modernism and the New Negro era's racial uplift. These contests paralleled the efforts of other "little magazines" such as *Poetry* and *The Dial*, which sponsored similar contests during the period (for example, in 1922 the $2,000 Dial Award went to T. S. Eliot for *The Waste Land*), and forged a collective identity for writers as well as an audience to receive their works. They also helped to formalize a pathway to publication for a host of African American writers, especially younger writers. Although racism and sexism circumscribed the extent to which, for Harlem Renaissance writers, "the literary prize could be a fast track to canonization," a process that Mark Morrison has suggested was the case for some of their white, usually male counterparts, *Crisis*'s and *Opportunity*'s prizes did direct the attention and resources of some supporters of racial uplift toward promising writers and their works.[3]

More than any other social forces, it was the circulation of funds from blacks as well as whites, and from individuals as much as institutions, that both marked and enabled the opportunities that Du Bois and Johnson described to their readers. Indeed, as David Levering Lewis has noted, "sponsoring talented Afro-Americans [had become] the rage" by the time *Crisis* and *Opportunity* announced their contests.[4] Harlem Renaissance sponsorship and patronage targeted not just the arts but education and business as well, and served to launch and sustain the careers of a number of African Americans who would contribute greatly to the period's accomplishments. While the Barnes and Harmon foundations, the Rosenwald Fund, and Amy and Joel Spingarn (through, for example, the NAACP Spingarn Medal) were representative of the "white capital and influence" that supported racial uplift and positioned the arts as an important site of its work, small business owners, fraternities and sororities, and individual patrons such as A'Lelia Walker and Casper Holstein were among the structures and sources of support in black civil society.[5]

With its interracial and dynamic character, such funding underscored the value of African American arts for which the editors argued. It also buttressed Du Bois's and Johnson's efforts to encourage black readers to read work of literary quality about themselves and to demonstrate that black writers were the most capable of writing such work. As just one specific instance of how *Crisis*'s and *Opportunity*'s literary contests came to occupy a central space in the period's culture of sponsorship and patronage, in the second year of *Crisis*'s contest Du Bois announced, "TO THE AUTHOR who the judges decide has written the best novel of Negro life, Messrs. Albert & Charles Boni, Inc., will pay outright as a Prize $1,000 in addition to the usual terms of royalty which will be arranged with the author," referring to the influential publishers who had recently published important works by African American authors, including Toomer's *Cane* and Fauset's *There Is Confusion*.[6] With such individual and institutional financial and social support for African American arts lending credibility to and increasing the visibility of the period's literary output, *Crisis* and *Opportunity* were well positioned to argue, as Johnson did, that "there is a curiosity about this life [in African America] as well as about the power of those who know it best to write about it."[7]

Opportunity's literary contests inspired palpable interest in "Negro life" and "writing by Negroes . . . free of deliberate propaganda and protest" while identifying as reciprocal and necessary both the writing and critical reading of the literature that the journal sought and published. This emphasis was central to the contests as a marketing strategy, but it also furthered the journal's work of shaping a New Negro reader. Although the processes developed by *Crisis* and *Opportunity* for hosting their literary contests differed less than the impact achieved through them, both journals' contests were concerted efforts at building a group literature through amassing high-quality writing. Together they underscored the fact that despite its interracial compass, the literary and artistic production that would become the Harlem Renaissance always entailed a search for African American writers and, as a consequence, a search for African American readers.

Reviewing the "Younger Literary Movement"

As Abby and Ronald Johnson have noted, "Where the contests differed between the rival magazines was in mood. Du Bois did a workmanlike job with his competitions. Johnson created an electric excitement."[8] This "electric excitement" began in the pages of *Opportunity*, especially as Johnson forged an editorial presence that galvanized a period-defining dynamism through the annual awards dinners that he hosted to showcase the talent that *Opportunity* was able to cultivate. Johnson's tactical advantage in announcing *Opportunity*'s contest before *Crisis*'s, and his diligence in getting aspiring writers to respond, facilitated *Opportunity*'s outreach and gave it a different appearance from that of Du Bois and *Crisis*. The similarities lay in the fact that both men used their respective journals to mentor aspiring writers and model ways to engage works produced at the moment of a self-proclaimed literary and arts renaissance. Nevertheless, the difference in mood was palpable, and Charles Johnson's sensibility was as central as Du Bois's in forging this distinction.

Through Johnson's editorship, the elements as he described them of a relevant and thriving journal focused on African American life—the "long list of valuable contributors," the "careful marshaling of scientific discussion," and the "literature and discussion of literature, refreshing poetry, critical book reviews, and attractive illustrations"—set the stage for *Opportunity*'s larger and, arguably, most important work: showcasing and celebrating the promise of African American writers.[9] As Johnson affirmed to *Opportunity*'s readers in January 1925, it was "possible to make the problems of Negro life intelligible by making them clear" and "to make Negro life interesting even for those who lack *a priori* sympathy for the under-dog, thru the charm and vitality of the emerging group of Negro writers."[10] Johnson's declarations underscored the journal's mission as an extension of the National Urban League, but they also highlighted the attention Johnson paid in the pages of *Opportunity* throughout his tenure to African American writers and the conditions that created them. His search for competent writers whose work would display such "charm and vitality" was a way to inspire confidence and achieve a permanent flow of literary output. The young writers that Johnson and *Opportunity* sought had potential, but as with the larger population they often came to represent, it was far from realized. Johnson intended to encourage pride in that potential and shape it into a commitment to develop.

In his "Note on the New Literary Movement" Johnson argued, "If this awakening is to be a sound, wholesome expression of growth rather than a fad to be discarded in a few seasons, it must somehow be preserved from the short-sighted exploiters of sentiment" and avoid "a double standard of competence as a substitute for the normal rewards of study and practice."[11] Here Johnson echoed Du Bois in content and to a degree in tone. Their editorials frequently detailed the implications of developing a cadre of capable African American writers and placing before the journals' readership evidence of their potential and growth. Johnson's and Du Bois's comments in this regard participated in shaping improved racial relations as much as they did in fostering racial pride. *Opportunity* echoed this sentiment in its coverage of the annual contests for 1925, 1926, and 1927, especially in reprinting judges' comments, prizewinning submissions, and, in a signal move similar to *Crisis*'s guest editorials on craft, key speeches delivered at each of the awards dinners. Here again the coverage had a practical purpose both in sustaining interest in the contests, so as to garner (more and better) submissions, and in reinforcing a point that Johnson relayed to *Opportunity*'s readers in August 1925: "There is no contention that Negro writers should not attempt to treat anything but Negro themes; rather that it is important *now* that Negro themes should be treated competently and that Negro writers, knowing them best, should be the ones to do it."[12]

An early and vocal advocate of African American writers' artistic autonomy, Johnson paired validation of representations of the diversity in African American life with a commitment to the mastery of craft; Du Bois would do the same in later years of *Crisis*'s contests. This dual focus recurred in the other components of *Opportunity*'s coverage of its annual contests. Although its inclusion of poetry and coverage of African American letters in earlier issues were precursors, *Opportunity*'s sponsorship of a literary contest still likely surprised its regular readers. After all, what did literature, not to mention cultivating writing talent, have to do with the National Urban League's attention to social conditions, especially as they influenced African American life? For Johnson, the reference to this "new period in creative expression among Negroes" clarified the seeming urgency of his announcement, and the ultimate goal of "interracial good will" which the Urban League championed as part of its mission provided an appropriate rationale.[13] As the ambitious editor wrote later in the lead editorial for the September 1924 issue, "There is extreme usefulness... in interpreting the life and longings and emotional experiences of the Negro people to their shrinking and spiritually alien neighbors; of flushing old festers of hate and disgruntlement by becoming triumphantly articulate; [and] of forcing the interest and kindred feeling of the world by sheer force of the humanness and beauty of one's own story."[14] This was his message, in part, to all of the journal's readers regardless of identity.

Because the burden of representation in this "interracial good will" was African Americans', Johnson courted this segment of *Opportunity*'s readership specifically through appeals to their racial affinity and their sense that achievement for one was the same as achievement for all. To *Opportunity*'s black readers, Johnson equally surmised that "the judgment of some of the foremost students of American literature offers encouragement for the future of imaginative writing by Negroes." Invoking a New Negro reader and identifying self-determination as a force for racial pride, Johnson asserted that "there is an opportunity now for Negroes themselves to replace their out-worn representations in fiction faithfully and incidentally to make themselves better understood."[15] Through the literary contest, then, Johnson's *Opportunity* would simultaneously cultivate African Americans as racially affirmed writers and readers. The merging of this cultural work through the contests was expedient, of course, but also made easier because several of the magazine's predecessors, particularly Du Bois's *Crisis*, had a long and influential history of situating the New Negro reader as one who read good literature and took note of its characteristics—a practice that both editors encouraged their aspiring writers to adopt.

For over a decade prior to *Opportunity*'s appearance as a journal, *Crisis* celebrated African American creativity and related achievements. Known as not only the NAACP's organ but also a forum for its visionary, passionate, and critical editor, *Crisis* targeted the "problem[s] of the color line" with acuity but also advanced public discussions about the importance of literacy and literature to African American life. A contributor himself, and a highly visible advocate of a New Negro reader and a corresponding literary culture, Du Bois articulated his enthusiasm for African America's arts and letters this way:

> *Crisis* has always stood for Truth,—the Truth when it is bitter, because we believe this is the only path to reform, for the Truth when it is sweet, for that heartens all. We shall continue to stand thus for the Truth. In addition to this we want to increase that part of our mission which, while not neglected, has had too little attention in the past, and that is the work of propagating and encouraging Beauty. We Negroes have gone fast forward in economic development, in political and social agitation; and we are likely to forget that the great mission of the Negro to America and the modern world is the development of Art and the appreciation of the Beautiful.[16]

CHAPTER 2

This preamble to the announcement of *Crisis*'s first contest in 1923, sponsored by the Delta Omega chapter of the African American sorority Alpha Kappa Alpha, relayed a conception of the role of art in African American life that Du Bois would champion—but with the qualification that "all art is propaganda and ever must be"—throughout the Harlem Renaissance.[17]

In striving for full citizenship and eradicating "the color line," Du Bois argued, African Americans would need to draw on their rich cultural and artistic resources. As he pointed out, African Americans had attended to "the development of Art and the appreciation of the Beautiful" but were far from realizing a full expression of their gifts in this regard. Through Du Bois's leadership, *Crisis* cultivated African America's artistic potential, through "picture and drawing, by fiction, essays, poetry, [and] by the organization of a Negro Institute of Literature and Art."[18] More than *Crisis*'s book reviews, columns, advertisements, and Du Bois's editorials, Jessie Fauset's appointment as literary editor in 1919 displayed the journal's cultural work in this regard. Fauset worked frequently and effectively, especially through *Crisis,* to sustain African Americans' creativity and respond to the interest in it that audiences showed during the period. Her reviews, particularly of their poetry, fiction, and drama, also contributed to the esteem in which Langston Hughes, for one, held her work.[19] Concurrent with her influential efforts as literary editor and mentor to young writers (within and beyond *Crisis*'s pages), Fauset was celebrated as an up-and-coming writer, even a standard-bearer for the "younger generation."

As Alain Locke remarked about her debut novel in "The Younger Literary Movement," a *Crisis* review article that he co-authored with Du Bois in 1924, "here in refreshing contrast with the bulk of fiction about the Negro, we have a novel of the educated and aspiring classes." For Locke, the exceptional quality of *There Is Confusion* lay in the fact that Fauset had "sketched a Negro group against a wide social background of four generations—almost as much perspective as can be gotten on any social group in America."[20] A few months later, writing for *Opportunity* Montgomery Gregory similarly celebrated Fauset's novel as the "first treatment in fiction of the educated strata of Negro urban life."[21]

Although these were just two reviews of the book, Locke's and Gregory's articles were part of a wave of literary criticism treating new African American literature that "older generation" black writers (and their white contemporaries, including Pearl Buck, Fannie Hurst, H. L. Mencken, and T. S. Stribling) offered the reading publics of early 1920s America.

George Schuyler declared himself one such reader in his review for *The Messenger,* a journal that covered literary matters during the period but did not host any contests. Schuyler noted that he "started reading [*There Is Confusion*] on a Sunday morning and finished its 297 pages before [he] went to bed," adding a more pointed assessment: "I trust the thousands of Negro book lovers will *buy* this book. If it is a *financial* success, there will be a widening field of opportunity for our rising group of young writers, struggling to express the yearnings, hopes, and aspirations of the race."[22]

Across these reviews, then, ran not only celebrations of individual talent and implications for (better) race relations, but also explicit syntheses of this literary output (and related social achievements such as the black women's club movement, the Niagara movement, and the Krigwa little theater movement) into a historic marker. Du Bois wrote commandingly about this dynamic when he surmised early in his review of Jean Toomer's *Cane* that "there are two books [the other being Fauset's *There Is Confusion*] before me, which, if I mistake not, will mark an epoch."[23]

Some reviewers celebrating the aspiring writers of the Harlem Renaissance attended as directly to quality as they did to racial firsts. In *Crisis*'s 1923 review of *Bronze,* Georgia Douglas Johnson's third volume of poetry, this attention was registered as the unnamed reviewer, likely Fauset, applauded Douglas Johnson's maturity as a "homecoming of mind and heart to intimately racial thought and experience." *Bronze* offered an instance of "readable poetry" that was "commendable" precisely because it "avoid[ed] sentimentality" yet did not succumb to "propaganda."[24]

Reviews that extolled and detailed such maturation appeared alongside others that framed the early 1920s as a period when a collective need was increasingly being left wanting. *Opportunity*'s review of Jean Toomer's *Cane* argued this point later that year. Reviewer Montgomery Gregory contended that "America has waited . . . for that native son who would avoid the pitfalls of propaganda and moralizing on the one hand

and the snares of a false and hollow race pride on the other hand." For Gregory, Toomer was "in a remarkable manner the answer to this call." Not surprisingly, praising *Cane* as meeting this collective need, racial and national, through deft handling of both nuanced racial representation and probing literary form implied a promise for the future. Echoing the sentiments of others about the role that writers and artists should embrace in the uplift of African America, Gregory concluded by stating: "*Cane* leaves this final message with me. In the South we have a 'powerful underground' race with a marvelous emotional power which like Niagara before it was harnessed is wasting itself. Release it into proper channels, direct its course intelligently, and you have possibilities for future achievement that challenge imagination. The hope of the race is in the great blind forces of the masses properly utilized by capable leaders."[25] Positioning himself as one such leader, Gregory read the artistry of both Toomer and *Cane* as evidence of this rich yet untapped "underground." It was Gregory's signal to the magazine's readers that more was to come.

Several reviews of this type appeared in the months prior to the announcements of *Crisis*'s and *Opportunity*'s contests and helped forge a public discourse that defined the reading and writing of good literature, especially about African America, as a form of service to the race. Frequently the qualities detailed in these reviews were directed specifically at African American readers as potential writers. Gregory, again, offered one of the more explicit statements in this regard. In reviewing *There Is Confusion* in June 1924 for *Opportunity*, he underscored the promise of this new generation. One role of the African American writer being "to see the life of the race artistically," he noted that "our writers of the younger school have been the first to catch this sound point of view and upon their strict adherence to it in the future depends the successful development of Negro art and literature." In this way Gregory reminded the aspiring poets, novelists, and playwrights among *Opportunity*'s readers that the future of African American literature was their province and that "treat[ing] our life as material to be objectively moulded [sic] into creations of beauty" was the necessary way to ensure it.[26]

Aware that such responsibility would weigh on the minds of these budding artists, Gregory expounded on his cultural formula, returning to Fauset and Toomer as examples of how it also produced individual achievement: "The success of writers such as Jessie Fauset and Jean Toomer is ample proof that true merit can surmount the barriers of race prejudice and that the doors of the literary world are at least ajar for the talented and ambitious youth of our race. Both of these writers also offer the lesson that the more ambitious works cannot be attained by sudden flight, but only by long and patient apprenticeship."[27]

What Gregory called young writers' attention to in this review Du Bois and Charles Johnson identified as an institutional practice and a basis for national outreach. Indeed, the literary contests sponsored by *Crisis* and *Opportunity* often functioned as a second stage in the "apprenticeship" of the kind of writer who, as famously envisioned by James Weldon Johnson, would "find a form that [would] express the racial spirit by symbols from within rather than by symbols from without."[28]

Apprenticing the New Negro Reader-Writer

Save for the absence of a featured work, the editorials and columns announcing *Opportunity*'s and *Crisis*' contests often read like the early reviews published in these journals' pages. They similarly characterize the 1920s as a viable moment for self-determination and literary production, the era's receptive reading public and publishing opportunities, its small but growing cadre of talent, and its array of new, individual and collective responses to America's racial character. Just as the reviews I have discussed had done, the submission guidelines both journals offered the reader-writers among their African American audience also linked the reflective study and creative production of the racial group's cultural store through individual experience and form with inducements promising artistic and monetary success. Immediately following Johnson's editorial in *Opportunity*'s September 1924 issue, potential "Negro contestants" encountered the list of prizes, which ranged from $30 up to $100 for first prize in each of the five categories: short story, poetry, play, essay, and "personal experience sketch." The pledge that "winning stories [would] be published" with a formal announcement at a "special meeting in New York" punctuated the notice.[29] With these incentives explicitly yet succinctly framing the "rules of the contest" which followed, Johnson's reader-writers were presented with criteria that, if met, would bolster their chances of winning and thereby uplifting the race as paid and published writers.

With the exception of poetry, these genre requirements reinforced a focus on African American life, directing potential entrants to render it palpably and formulaically. In the essay category, for example, *Opportunity* informed readers that "the object here is simply to bid for a much abused type of literary expression, in the hope of finding some examples of recognizable literary merit." What would garner recognition as possessing literary merit, then, were entries that "str[ove] for clarity of diction, forcefulness, and originality of ideas, logical structure, deft and effective employment of language, accuracy of data, and economy of words." But such entries would be recognized as doing so only if, the contest rules concluded, the essay's subject "relate[d] directly or indirectly to Negro life and contacts, or situations in which Negroes have a conspicuous interest."[30] By pairing racial focus with formal qualities, even rendering the former as the most essential component of the latter, *Opportunity* reinforced the idea that the *best* American writing could both come from within and be about African America. Regardless of whether or not *Opportunity*'s black readers merely read previously published works or began creating new work based on them, these contest rules extended the journal's practice of forging an interracial audience by appealing to white readers while addressing African Americans, at times with greater familiarity and authority, elevating reading and writing literature by and about African Americans into newsworthy practices.

Crisis's detailed announcement of its own contest a month later read similarly to *Opportunity*'s. Because *Opportunity*'s "publicity of its prize offer" had come first, Du Bois noted, *Crisis* had decided to "put the date of [its] competition well on in the spring" to avoid "unnecessary rivalry."[31] Du Bois directed potential entrants to make note of the contest's time frame, conditions, and prize and publication incentives. In the same genres as well as for illustrations, *Crisis*'s first-prize amounts ranged from $100 for fiction to $50 (the lowest) for both essays and verse.[32] He anticipated a cadre of winners.

In addition, Du Bois linked the journal's contests to the development of the period's "little theater movement," or Krigwa. Du Bois not only chronicled its history in *Crisis* but also linked its programming with the contests. For example, he noted in the guidelines for the third contest, in 1927, that "persons who have received two first or second prizes in any class of entries will not be eligible to enter the contest but will be named as members of the Krigwa Academy and may be asked to serve as judges."[33] This reciprocity had a practical purpose in sustaining African American art and artistry. As he observed in his 1926 chronicle of Krigwa, "five years ago there were practically no plays that filled the specifications noted," that is, of building "a real folk-play movement of American Negroes." But, he added, "the situation has begun to change on account of the prizes offered by CRISIS magazine and other agencies for other reasons."[34]

As these links demonstrate, Du Bois did not simply echo *Opportunity*'s format in announcing *Crisis*'s contests, especially in giving potential contestants guidance by detailing benefits and procedures. Du Bois borrowed *Opportunity*'s recognizable form but went beyond its announcement as a form of instruction in the craft of racial representation. Whereas *Opportunity* stressed the need for "recognizable literary merit" as a service to the race and offered a few examples in this vein, *Crisis* augmented its own announcement with detailed guest editorials on the literary genres covered by its contests. This move to have experts detail the elements of craft followed Fauset's earlier critique of the nineteen submissions for the 1923 short story contest, of which "twelve were plotless, three possessed slight plot, two started off with the makings of a good plot . . . and the last, the prizewinner, was built around a plot slightly less strong," and her subsequent contention that "masterpieces are the compositions which have been worked at, thrown aside, picked up again, despaired over, cut and slashed and mended and sworn at."[35] The instruction in craft also gave additional texture to the idea that the contest was conceived not just to inspire the creatively inclined but also to turn readers into writers.

This goal was precisely what Du Bois's guest contributor Mark Seyboldt articulated in November 1924 through his "About the Short Story." Seyboldt's concluding comments make this point well. "To all beginners,"

CHAPTER 2

he wrote, "the way to learn to write is to write. [*Crisis*'s] prizes are to encourage writers: those who have written, those who are writing, and those who have always thought they might like to. Let everybody try. Hunt the old story that is hidden away and furbish it up. Unfold again the story that has been rejected by all the editors, so long as it has not yet been published; or take from the recesses of your mind the story that has long been tingling there and waiting to be born."[36] As much as it underscored the contest's role as a vehicle for making potential entrants' writing tangible, even publishable, Seyboldt's turn to direct address here spoke urgently to *Crisis*'s readers, compelling them to see themselves as writers. Conveying this inspiration *to write* was not Seyboldt's only intention, of course. Through "About the Short Story," Seyboldt set out to define the genre and impart a method for its effective construction. In doing so, he projected the New Negro reader as a potential New Negro writer. This projection informed how both *Crisis* and *Opportunity* chronicled their contests, from announcements through to the publication of prizewinning submissions.

For Seyboldt, this entailed both an appeal to potential writers' commitment to study and a response to their need for practical examples. And "for a clear conception of what the short story could be, naturally nothing is better than reading the best models." To inspire and instruct, he excerpted Edgar Allan Poe's review of Nathaniel Hawthorne's *Twice-Told Tales*, isolating Poe's definition of the genre and offering *Crisis*'s readers the actual words of exemplars. Seyboldt specifically included the famed writer's assertion that through the "short prose narrative" the "reader is at the writer's control." After developing this "introduction," Seyboldt related a history of the genre, drawing from several sources—ranging from practical guides such as *Materials and Methods of Fiction* to selections from the *Critic*'s 1897 list of the "12 best American short stories"—for subsequent study. He reinforced the message of the contest announcement and courted *Crisis*'s African American readers by offering his own instance of racial representation, writing, "We are proud to know that among the masters of the short-story in the United States is our own Charles Chesnutt, and those who would study the art of short-story writing as applied to the American Negro should by all means read 'The

Conjure Woman' and 'The Wife of His Youth.' "[37] In doing so, Seyboldt supported *Crisis*'s efforts to garner quality submissions and responded, if only rhetorically, to the less confident and those for whom racism had stunted their belief in their abilities. In pointing to Chesnutt, Seyboldt offered proof not just of what was possible but even of the mastery that one could achieve.

With Seyboldt's perspectives in "About the Short Story," Du Bois featured another advocate for paying dual attention to craft and racial representation (for placing in the contest and for the future of African American letters) in the work of potential entrants.[38] Given the months that transpired between the announcement of the contest and the publication of the winning entries, this strategy facilitated consistent coverage of the contest, which was intended to boost the number and quality of submissions. Although it does not appear that Seyboldt served as a judge for submissions to the contest genres on which he offered notes, his presence and expert perspectives exemplified *Crisis*'s practice of publishing the words of prominent figures to lend credibility to the journal's contests and achieve visibility for them. This was a signal element driving the idea behind the contests from their inception.

If *Crisis*'s guest editorials on the craft of the contests' genres served this function in a marked way, so did the inclusion of judges' comments (on the quality of submissions in general and prizewinning pieces in particular) as features in the journal. Before addressing how *Crisis* displays its judges' commentary as a means of articulating and reinforcing the need for both craft and racial representation in writing submissions to the contest and then in reading the winning entries, I want to turn to famed writer Charles Chesnutt's letter to Du Bois after he judged the short story portion of the 1925 contest. As Chesnutt noted in his letter, quality in a story depended on four elements: "1, the theme; 2, the plot and its working out; 3, the language, including the style; [and] 4, the effect on the reader." Chesnutt not only foregrounded "the effect on the reader" as an essential element of a good story but also noted three categories of actual readers: "a colored reader"; "an editor reading [a given submission] with a view to publication"; and, a reader who operated somewhere between but, arguably, shared qualities with these others.[39]

CHAPTER 2

In his role as a judge, and from his experiences reading and writing as first among a small number of successful and celebrated African American writers, the way Chesnutt read the four stories that *Crisis* forwarded to him suggested that he was, or that his reading practices were, a composite of all three types. Such a suggestion emerges from the brief notations that he offered on each submission. His acknowledgment that two of the stories—"Three Dogs and a Rabbit" and "High Yaller"—were "well-written" reflected the viewpoints of all three types of readers, though arguably this was a quality that an editor would be more likely to emphasize—in other words *read for*—than the other kinds of readers. Chesnutt signaled the challenges that might have faced a reader of "Easy Pickin's," noting, "A dialect which is so difficult that the reader has to stop to figure out what it means detracts from the interest of the story, in which respect this writer sins."[40]

By contrast, "High Yaller" compelled Chesnutt to question the authenticity of the story's racial representation with the remark "I have never yet met knowingly a fair colored girl who wanted to be darker. The almost universal desire is, as the advertising pages of the colored newspapers and periodicals bear witness, to get as much whiter as possible. So the story is not convincing." As for "There Never Fell a Night So Dark," the story that he found befitting first place, Chesnutt appeared to see in it more than its publishable quality, racial appeal, and translatability. Because of its "human theme," Chesnutt remarked, "the little story touches the emotions and to that extent meets the essential requirement of a good story."[41] Although he was only one of four judges for the fiction category in the 1925 competition—H. G. Wells, Sinclair Lewis, and Mary White Ovington were the others—the awards most closely reflected Chesnutt's rankings, although his first and second choices finished in reverse order.

In excerpting the letter, Du Bois made Chesnutt's work as a New Negro reader visible to the journal's readership. In doing so, he delivered on an advertised benefit of participating in the competition and underscored the integrity of the contest afforded by the interracial group of judges. Although Du Bois printed excerpts from the letters written by two of the other judges—Wells, who, he noted, was "perhaps the foremost novelist of the world," and Lewis, whom he distinguished as "the most popular contemporary American novelist"—it was Chesnutt's comments about Rudolph Fisher's "High Yaller" that Du Bois featured prominently in the "Words of Judges" section of the column announcing the winners.[42] It is difficult to know precisely why Du Bois quoted from Chesnutt's letter at length, though he likely had practical (Chesnutt provided the most commentary about the first-place submission) as well as ideological reasons (privileging the words of "our own laureate" as a tangible instance of racial pride). Whatever his reasons, the attention to craft and racial representation that characterized the excerpt from Chesnutt's letter and on which Du Bois focused are especially instructive.

Printed alongside Joel Spingarn's statement that the essays he judged were "charged with feeling, personal feeling rooted in the race feeling," Chesnutt's comments about "High Yaller" singled out the skilled use of "language and figures of speech" and its likely "reflection[s] of Negro life in Harlem."[43] Chesnutt's comments worked with those of the other judges to reinforce a central motivation for the contest that Du Bois routinely noted in announcements detailing contest guidelines and later reasserted in 1926. Du Bois charged potential entrants:

> Write then about things as you know them; be honest and sincere. In CRISIS at least, you do not have to confine your writings to the portrayal of beggars, scoundrels and prostitutes; you can write about ordinary decent colored people if you want. On the other hand do not fear the Truth. Plumb the depths. If you want to paint Crime and Destitution and Evil paint it. Do not try to be simply respectable, smug, conventional. Use propaganda if you want. Discard it and laugh if you will. But be true, be sincere, be thorough, and do a beautiful job.[44]

In beginning his editorial by telling his readers to "write then about things as you know them," he implied that such personal knowledge was a requirement for successful writing as well.

More important, Du Bois signaled to prospective entrants the journal's openness to a diversity of themes regarding African American life. Mindful of the growing calls for autonomy coming from the younger generation of writers in these crucial years of the Harlem Renaissance (Langston

Hughes published "The Negro Artist and the Racial Mountain" in 1926), Du Bois sought to boost submissions, especially in the context of *Opportunity*'s success at garnering a greater diversity of genres and entrants as well as a larger number of submissions. Du Bois also placed before *Crisis*'s readers the idea that thoroughness of craft and sincerity in racial representation were key criteria on which submissions would be read and judged. Indeed, the judges' comments that both *Crisis* and *Opportunity* printed following their contests echoed William Stanley Braithwaite's encouragement of "technical command to achieve a notable visionary expression." This was especially true with the awards announcement for *Opportunity*'s second contest, also known as the Casper Holstein prizes, in June 1926. Johnson provided readers a "view of the comments from those undoubted authorities in American letters on the technical excellencies [sic] and failings of the entries submitted" in his editorial for the issue. He then excerpted responses from judges' opinions of the poetry submissions and noted the journal's intention to do the same, in subsequent issues, for the remaining genres.[45]

Braithwaite, for example, described Lucy Ariel Williams's "Northboun' " as "a fulfillment of Matthew Arnold's conception of poetry as a 'criticism of life' as applied to dialect currently used." In doing so, he suggested that dialect was one way to represent African American experience, and read Williams's poem as the successful merger of form and subject that *Opportunity*'s contests called for and celebrated.[46] Affirmation of this success worked in three ways. First, *Opportunity* positioned Braithwaite, an influential African American poet-critic, as an authoritative New Negro reader. By juxtaposing Braithwaite's and James Weldon Johnson's reviews with those of their white counterparts, in this case Robert Frost's remarks, the display of judges' comments validated Braithwaite's influence as it documented the interracial collaboration to which the National Urban League was committed—and the journal's own success at it. The echoes of Braithwaite's praise of Williams's successful merging of styles found in the four other judges' comments are particularly important. They gave voice to the idea that African American life was an appropriate subject not just for poetry but for good, even the best, American poetry. For *Opportunity*'s enterprising editor, such marshaling of proof, through the judges' comments and the entries themselves, pointed "to a new social consciousness just as surely as [it] point[ed] to a new literary technique."[47]

Readers Respond

When Charles Johnson concluded his June 1926 *Opportunity* editorial by asserting that Braithwaite's and the other judges' comments "reflect[ed] descriptive judgments which may be easily confirmed on a reading of the poems themselves," it was one of several indications, both direct and indirect, that the contests and their implications for African American life targeted an engaged readership.[48] Implying that *Opportunity*'s readers were discerning and resourceful, Johnson invited them to verify the judges' evaluations for themselves. His encouragement to read the winning submissions marked Johnson's familiarity with his readers while suggesting that the premises of the contest—from his claims about the timeliness of the journal's literary competition to a prominent writer's declarations about the elements of a "good" poem—not to mention the winning submissions themselves, were open to debate and intended to solicit a response.

Pragmatically, Johnson sought such responses and wrote frequently about the letters he received from readers who desired to become published writers themselves, from inquiries about contest rules to requests for feedback on potential themes and story ideas. Actual submissions, quality submissions, were the real measures of response, and of *Opportunity*'s success. Across the years when the journal was sponsoring its contests, Johnson noted the number of submissions and commented on their quality. "We announce the Second Annual *Opportunity* Contest for Negro writers," he proclaimed in October 1925, "with increased awards and extended departments. The first experiment in the field of literature netted conspicuous and pleasing results. It located about 800 Negroes scattered through nearly every state in the union, the great majority of whom can express themselves effectively in prose and verse, and some of whom give promise of definite accomplishment in the field of letters."[49] Although the second and third years of the contest drew fewer entrants, though not substantially so, Johnson pointed to the hundreds of submissions as evidence that the contests had "stimulate[d] not merely an interest in Negro life and in the work of artists of the race, but work of a character which stands firmly and without apology along with that of any other race."[50]

In this way, he reasoned in his editorials, the contests forged both racial pride and uplift. *Opportunity*'s textual mirroring of the most representative, generically proficient, even innovative, and expertly judged creative work from African America was a practice that any of the journal's readers—black or white—could experience and thereby derive a sense of pride. Equally important, the evidence of the contests' success—in terms of numbers of entrants, the willing participation of an interracial mix of writers, some of them quite well known, and the winning submissions themselves—countered stereotypes (or at least were poised to do so) that worked to keep racism normative and interracial exchange limited.

With the increased quality of *Opportunity*'s winning submissions, the contests, especially in the second and third years, also suggested that entrants had embraced the writing guides and judges' comments, at least to some degree. For some, their entries represented a first experience of putting such instruction into practice; for others the guidance supplemented their own natural gifts and/or prior training. Although his immediate goal was to motivate more submissions, Johnson clearly understood how printing winning entries alongside representative comments from contest judges could inspire engaged readers to employ the criteria specified by the judges in their individual and collective reading.

As a characteristic feature of his editorials for *Crisis,* Du Bois also wrote frequently and directly to readers about their role as the journal's partners and the actions he believed they should undertake in this moment of racial uplift and interracial cooperation. Participation in the magazine's literary contests—whether as an entrant or simply by reading winning submissions in order to increase their awareness of the race's advancement—was a component of the cultural self-education that Du Bois advocated, especially for African American readers, throughout *Crisis*'s pages. In letters to the editor features, specifically "The Outer Pocket," Du Bois printed reader reactions to the journal's content, race relations in America and globally, and his editorials. A 1926 letter from a reader named Elizabeth Leonard displays an almost personal familiarity with Du Bois, mirroring the tone he adopted in his editorials. The letter is typical of the correspondence that Du Bois printed. Leonard wrote: "As president of a women's club, I am writing to you for information in regard to your views on race assimilation, intermarriage of Negroes and whites. We have just completed a two weeks' study of your book 'Souls of Black Folk' and are unable to arrive at a definite conclusion as to your attitude toward this question."[51]

Du Bois offered a five-point reply that reinforced his bond with Leonard and her fellow club members as engaged *Crisis* readers but that also sought to focus their attention on, and even their structured study of, important ideas circulating in both the private and public spheres. He responded directly—"usually, for obvious reasons, marriages within the group are most likely to be happy"—then elaborated on his opinion, adding, "Despite the above [perspective] I maintain the perfect right of any individual of any race, who is sane and normal, to marry the person who wishes to marry him."[52] Both as a direct reply to the members of this club and a means of engaging with *Crisis*'s larger readership, Du Bois's comments documented the seriousness with which he regarded the matter of intermarriage as much as they validated these women's engaged reading of *Souls* and *Crisis*.

Although Du Bois does not make explicit his rationale for selecting the letters he chose to print, a survey of them suggests a recurring effort to achieve some degree of balance between those that were critical and those that offered praise, though the majority of them addressed *Crisis*'s content and the work of the NAACP.[53] An anonymous letter that Du Bois printed in November 1926 reflected these elements and worked to underscore, even if indirectly, the purpose and importance of the contests, which aimed to cultivate young and emerging African American writers. Apologizing for writing out of "sheer presumptuousness," the anonymous writer noted, "In reading a recent issue of CRISIS, the article 'The Negro in Art' interested me very much, so much, in fact, that I find myself constantly reading and re-reading it."[54] The writer's admission exemplified the kind of New Negro reader that *Crisis* targeted and worked to cultivate through its content. It also reinforced the attention to African Americans' artistic production that the period's public discourse fostered. In its entirety, the letter voiced the concerns of a novice author trying to navigate the challenges of creating art in an America where racism was ever present.

The writer's concluding remarks brought those challenges into focus but also conveyed resilience. "There is a great deal of prejudice against Negro writers," this young writer observed, "even if the best authorities do persist in claiming that Art knows no colorline." Much of *Crisis*'s advocacy of African America's art made the same point, and the adoption of the literary contests was an effort to redress the prejudice that the writer noted. The contests were also designed to bolster young writers' confidence and to offer an alternative, supportive community as well as a venue for publication. Although the writer does not refer to *Crisis*'s contests explicitly, his determination echoed an attitude that Du Bois encouraged in potential entrants. "I am merely struggling now for a foothold in this world of Literature," the anonymous writer acknowledged. "Some day when I reach a certain pinnacle in the ladder of success and when I can afford to be optional and follow my own inclinations I am going to write great stories of great Negroes with great racial themes. Yes, some day. I am still young, being only twenty-two."[55] This determination and ambition were precisely what Du Bois wanted potential entrants to possess.

Of course, not all of *Crisis*'s readers became entrants in the journal's literary contests. Du Bois clearly courted readers as well as would-be writers. One letter printed in the April 1927 issue offered a pointed response to the winning submissions to the contests. Identifying herself as a *Crisis* reader who "enjoys everything [in the journal] with one exception," Ethel Johnson expressed her dissatisfaction with the "so-called 'prize stories'" such as Rudolph Fisher's "High Yaller" (which she incorrectly called "The Yaller Gal") and first-time winner Edmund Shean's "The Death Game," which, respectively, won first prize in 1925 and second prize in the 1926 contest. Johnson described them as "deplorable" and leveled the charge that the contests did not foster the type of racial representation that she and other African American readers thought desirable. Johnson was "puzzled to know why young authors of today can find nothing along the lines of decency in the race, to write about." Lamenting the prevalence of stories that featured none of the "beautiful Negro women, old and young" who might "inspire the higher ideals of life," she offered a plea: "Just for a change please select something of this type."[56]

Given Du Bois's expression of similar concerns prior to and during the contests, it is not surprising that he printed Johnson's comments. Even if her critique was directed at the judges as much as it was toward the "young authors," as she called them, it still served to advance Du Bois's arguments about the need for more affirming, middle-class depictions of African American life. In this respect Ethel Johnson asked, with even greater urgency and anger, a version of the question that Du Bois had posed in launching the symposium "The Negro in Art: How Shall He Portrayed?" a year earlier: "Is there not a real danger that young colored writers will be tempted to follow the popular trend in portraying Negro character in the underworld rather than seeking to paint the truth about themselves and their own social class?"[57] Johnson's letter read as a definitive "yes!" Its appearance in *Crisis* validated the perspective of an individual New Negro reader—a perspective that several respondents to the symposium rejected in favor of artistic autonomy—and made another case for the necessity and potential of the literary contests. Although they would end just a few years later—the result of a combination of limited funds, the demands of other intra- and interracial priorities, and, despite the editors' and journals' best efforts, the fact that the submissions still had, as Charles Johnson noted, "some distance to go"—*Crisis*'s and *Opportunity*'s literary contests sought, engaged, and cultivated a continuum of New Negro readers and turned the effort into a public and national affair.[58]

Reading *Crisis*'s and *Opportunity*'s literary contests comparatively helps illustrate the commonalities between them as well as the distinctions. As several scholars have shown, these dynamics reflected Du Bois's and Charles Johnson's personalities as much as the seemingly ever-changing developments informing and propelling the Harlem Renaissance.[59] Although Du Bois and Johnson (and by extension the contests they oversaw) approached the use of literature as a tool for racial uplift differently, there were important similarities. In terms of the contests, perhaps the most important similarity was the motivation for offering them in the first place. Both Du Bois and Johnson recognized the second decade of the twentieth century as an opportune time for realizing African America's artistic and literary potential. As the contests featured in *Crisis* and *Opportunity* demonstrated, a number of writers possessed and realized that potential during and beyond the period of the Harlem Renaissance. In *Opportunity*'s first, 1925 contest, winners included E. Franklin Frazier for his essay "Social Equality and the Negro," Langston Hughes for his poem "The Weary Blues," Zora Neale Hurston for her short story "Spunk" and her play "Colored Struck," and Countee Cullen for his poems "To One Who Said Me Nay" and "A Song of Sour Grapes."[60]

While some of these writers would go on to win subsequent contests, others would secure contracts to publish their work, as was the case for Hughes, whose first volume of poetry, *Weary Blues,* was published by Alfred Knopf in 1926. Similarly in *Crisis,* winning writers' submissions marked the first of many accomplishments. In announcing the winners, *Crisis* reminded potential entrants among its readership that "prizes are the least valuable part of a prize contest."[61] For Eulalie Spence, whose play *Foreign Mail* won the 1926 drama contest, there was not only the prize and the announcement but also a performance of her play at the awards celebration at the International House in New York. Spence also benefited from a long and productive relationship with the Krigwa Players. A highlight of that relationship came a year later, when their production of her play *Fool's Errand* won the Samuel French Award at the Annual National Little Theater Tournament.[62] Although Johnson's contests achieved more immediate benefits in terms of bolstering African American artistry than did Du Bois's, for young writers especially, they both read African American life as a venue for transforming art, not to mention race relations, in 1920s America and frequently inspired their readers to do the same.

Though interracial in nature, *Crisis*'s and *Opportunity*'s literary contests were also part of the expression of racial pride that defined the period and, as a result, were explicit inducements for such racial identification. Hailing New Negro readers as he often did through direct address and providing opportunities to reply, Du Bois structured the *Crisis* contests as an exchange that would yield tangible benefits for African Americans and race relations generally and working writers in particular. Far from the only ways that the Harlem Renaissance achieved such goals, *Crisis*'s and *Opportunity*'s literary contests sustained a specific focus on the need to support and develop writers. They compelled readers to appreciate and engage the "poems and stories of promising writers from remote literary centers . . . [who were] hidden away behind their timidities and doubts" precisely because they "revealed a marvelous comprehension of life, and a facility and charm in expressing themselves."[63]

This revelation underscored how African Americans supported but also authorized the potential of these writers. After declaring *Opportunity*'s first contest a success in many respects, Charles Johnson added, "For the benefit of those who desire to read for their own entertainment and profit from the offerings of the most promising of these writers[,] we shall carry, after the prize winning manuscripts, certain of those which achieved honorable mention, and which were in competition for the place of highest rank. The work of the contest is just beginning."[64] Although short-lived with regard to the contests, the work of encouraging the practices of a New Negro reader that Johnson suggested here took several forms. Central among them was the effort to strengthen writers' engagement with other African Americans as readers and to advance the literary tradition that facilitated such bonds.

BEYOND *THE NEW NEGRO*
Artistry, Audience, and the Harlem Renaissance Literary Anthology

◆▶◆

Among its other features, Harlem Renaissance print culture documented a number of efforts to produce quality books about African America that every "Negro should have at his hand." The NAACP's *Crisis* made this work an explicit component of its advocacy throughout the period. "The Crisis Advertiser" in the May 1924 issue, for example, featured a special offer whereby, in exchange for two year-long subscriptions at the cost of three dollars, a *Crisis* reader could receive a copy of Booker T. Washington's *Up from Slavery* "beautifully printed and handsomely bound in English Red Leather."[1] The importance of this special offer resided not only in a reader's opportunity to own and exhibit a material register of culture and class status, as encoded in the "English Red Leather," but also in the way it furthered the idea of a New Negro reader through its selection of Washington's autobiography as an appropriate choice for building one's home library.

The "Crisis Advertiser" marketed this aspirational edition of *Up from Slavery* as an American *and* an African American classic. Its purchase would increase a reader's reverence for the "Wizard from Tuskegee," in the wake of his recent death in 1915, and encourage him or her to purchase other new works in this developing canon. The same edition of "The Crisis Advertiser" included other such works as Carter G. Woodson's *The Negro in Our History*, described as the "most useful book on the Negro," Robert Kerlin's "epoch-making" *Negro Poets and Their Poems*, and "one of the greatest books ever written on the Negro," J. A. Rogers's *From "Superman" to Man*.[2] Reflecting the perspectives of Du Bois as one of the foremost proponents of Africa's contributions to the world's civilization, the text advertising these books celebrated the ideals of culture as operating—beyond Europe and its descendants—among the world's "darker races." Each advertisement also signaled that *Crisis*'s readers were interested in the best works worth reading about the race and promoted these works as affordable, racially affirming, and accessible either by mail or from local booksellers.

It was not surprising to find advertisements for or reviews of an anthology such as Kerlin's *Negro Poets and Their Poems* in the period's journals and newspapers. By 1923, when the volume was published, literary anthologies had become representative of books of quality from and about African America. They also served as important vehicles for simultaneously targeting and constructing a New Negro reader, in this case "as an intelligent human being who wish[ed] to preserve the thought and experience of the world and of [her] own people."[3] To forge this desired outcome through a collection of poems, short stories, or plays, an editor had to produce an engaging work that inspired reading. A poet and contributing writer to *Opportunity* magazine, Frank Horne, affirmed these qualities in a review of some of the earliest literary anthologies to feature the work of African American writers. In his "Black Verse," Horne assessed Newman Ivey White and Walter Clinton Jackson's *Anthology of Verse by American Negroes*, noting that "the work is scholarly, and the treatment is both critical and sympathetic to some degree."[4]

Horne nevertheless declared that "the anthology is also sluggish; it lacks distinction and verve. It possesses neither the vigor and raciness of Professor Talley's folk lore collection [*Negro Folk Rhymes*], nor the poetical finesse and judgment of James Weldon Johnson's 'Book of American Negro Poetry.' The book lacks, in a sense, personality. To a student of the subject, the work is undeniably a worthy contribution; but to the reader of verse, it is a volume he can as well get along without."[5] Only one of numerous such volumes to appear between 1910 and 1940, White and Jackson's *Anthology* participated in efforts to chronicle African Americans' literary tradition and render it tangible. Horne's review reflected parallel commentary on the cultural work of these volumes, especially, as Horne noted, on how editors designed and presented them and the effect of those choices on readers. In Horne's estimation, the literary anthology should not only display dynamic literary texts but also be dynamic itself. Such qualities were viewed as necessary for the fusion of critical and creative frameworks that, for Horne, White and Jackson attempted but did not achieve. As a central marker of racial integrity and progress at the height of the Harlem Renaissance, anthologizing literature became an increasingly complicated cultural practice. Nowhere was this truer than in the pages of Alain Locke's volume *The New Negro*.

In "The Book That Launched the Harlem Renaissance," Arnold Rampersad has argued: "To many of the scholars and critics of the movement known as the Harlem Renaissance—that dramatic upsurge of creativity in literature, music, and art within black America that reached its zenith in the second half of the 1920s—*The New Negro* is its definitive text, its bible. The book, an anthology, represents the triumph of its compiler's vision of a community and a nation changing before its eyes."[6] To align *The New Negro*'s function as an anthology with its impact as arguably *the* canonical Harlem Renaissance text as Rampersad does allows for a consideration of its canonicity, which John Guillory reminds us "is not the property of the work itself but of its transmission, its relation to other works in a collocation of works."[7] *The New Negro*'s role in fostering the early careers of younger writers and visual artists, amplifying the status of more established writers, and launching the Harlem Renaissance also illustrated its canonical force.

Although mid- to late-twentieth-century retrospectives and critical discussions predominate as evidence of *The New Negro*'s canonicity, anthologies that built on the model it proffered also confirmed its status, as Guillory suggests, especially in the way they constituted responses to the manner in which *The New Negro* introduced writers as artists and strategically infused their perspectives into explicit and implicit models for reading African American literature and culture.[8] In what follows, I argue that three important anthologies to do so were Charles Johnson and the National Urban League's *Ebony and Topaz* (1927), Countee Cullen's *Caroling Dusk* (1927), and Otelia Cromwell, Lorenzo Dow Turner, and Eva Beatrice Dykes's *Readings from Negro Authors* (1931). As anthologies, they blended the contemporaneous developments of both similar and contrasting literary styles and themes within one or across multiple genres into the anthological tradition that *The New Negro* galvanized. Through them, readers were positioned to experience a work of literature as more than a racial first. In the pages of these anthologies, a Jessie Fauset story or a Langston Hughes poem was to live on as the creation of an artist and as a work of art.

Artistry in *The New Negro*

Brent Hayes Edwards has recently addressed the more than forty anthologies to appear throughout the Harlem Renaissance period and contended that "to note this flood of energy in modern print culture is to raise the question of the particular way an anthology frames race, the particular way it articulates an epistemology of blackness."[9] A more celebrated anthological "exhibition of blackness," especially for its ethnic and interracial appeal, than its predecessors, *The New Negro* was a cause célèbre—an uncommon feat for an anthology chronicling African American life and culture in the early twentieth century.[10] *The New Negro* was the product of turning the *Survey Graphic*'s "Harlem number" into a national text and liaison between the races. Given the increased focus on black cultural arts when it appeared in 1925, *The New Negro* was a well-timed and tightly coordinated effort on Locke's part to harness interest, particularly among white Americans and Europeans, in African Americans—their words, music, and visual arts. As he urged in the volume's foreword, "Whosoever wishes to see the Negro in his essential traits, in the full perspective of his achievement and possibilities, must seek the enlightenment of that self-portraiture which present developments of Negro culture are offering."[11]

With the volume, Locke broadened accounts of this development

CHAPTER 3

captured by the period's "race literature" and "race journalism" to what he described as "a national and even international scope."[12] More important, Locke fashioned *The New Negro* as a "stage" for "the Negro to speak for himself" on a range of issues. A signal formulation of artistry—what William Stanley Braithwaite referred to as the "passion and sympathy for life, its hurts, its sympathies, its desires, its joys, its defeats and stranger yearnings," and the ability to write "without the surrender or the compromise of the artist's vision"—wove the pages of *The New Negro* together.[13] It was a compelling framework for fostering relationships between black writers and their readers.

In *The New Negro*, Locke merged his *Survey Graphic* piece "Enter the New Negro" with a framing essay simply titled "Harlem" to create "The New Negro" and positioned it as the opening selection in the volume. This essay appealed to a diverse audience while constructing a provocative image of African American artists as New Negroes. In it Locke affirmed his commitment to the arts and letters in *The New Negro*, as opposed to a predominantly social-scientific focus. "In the last decade," he wrote, "something beyond the watch and guard of statistics has happened in the life of the American Negro and the three norns who have traditionally presided over the Negro problem have a changeling in their laps. The Sociologist, the Philanthropist, and the Race-leader are not unaware of the New Negro, but they are at a loss to account for him." If the reader was in any doubt as to who this model New Negro was, Locke made it explicit through the anthology generally and in this lead essay in particular, observing that from "the life-attitudes and self-expression of the Young Negro, in his poetry, his art, his education and his new outlook ... comes the promise and warrant of a new leadership." To reinforce his point, Locke quoted Langston Hughes's poem "Youth" in its entirety in his essay and printed it again in the volume's poetry section. As members of "the younger generation [that came], bringing its gifts," Hughes and his contemporaries, according to Locke, offered "the first fruits of the Negro Renaissance. [This] youth speaks, and the voice of the New Negro is heard."[14]

Such signaling was a trademark of Locke's volume. His essay "Negro Youth Speaks" opened with the statement "Here [in the foregoing pages] we have Negro youth, with arresting visions and vibrant prophecies; forecasting in the mirror of art what we must see and recognize in the streets of reality tomorrow, foretelling in new notes and accents the maturing speech of full racial utterance."[15] Both a pivotal framing narrative and an instance of his adroit editorializing, Locke's imaging of young African American artists, especially emerging poets, as the most influential New Negroes exemplified Locke's role as a celebrant of artistry in African America.

In addition, Locke echoed his introductory point about the degree of self-determination fueling African American identity. He argued: "Our poets have now stopped speaking for the Negro—they speak as Negroes. Where formerly they spoke to others and tried to interpret, they now speak to their own and try to express. They have stopped posing, being nearer the attainment of poise." For Locke, this capacity for dynamic self-expression was especially significant because, he asserted, "by the evidence and promise of the cultured few, we are at last spiritually free, and offer through art an emancipating vision to America."[16] Through pronouncements such as these realizing the thematic core of *The New Negro*, Locke's reading of artistry reverberated as an early and, given the volume's contemporaneous acclaim, a celebrated assertion of artistic freedom.

Reviewing *The New Negro*

Between 1925 and 1926 at least twelve reviews of Locke's volume appeared in print.[17] A frequent contributor and longtime NAACP Detroit branch spokesperson, Robert Bagnall reviewed *The New Negro* for the National Urban League's *Opportunity* in February 1926. He contended that the anthology "convinces its readers that the New Negro is and that he possesses gifts which the world must recognize." For Bagnall these gifts operated in both the "reading matter" and the "physical side of the book," which together made the "volume a valuable possession—one to be treasured." In detailing its structure, Bagnall inscribed *The New Negro* further as a work of art and about artists: "Here we see the genius of Jean Toomer and the technique of Rudolph Fisher; here we experience the beauty of Countee Cullen, the bitterness of [Claude] McKay, the sophisticated

CHAPTER 3

abandon of Langston Hughes and the revealing imagery of James Weldon Johnson."[18] Notwithstanding Bagnall's gendered reading of artistry, his account suggests some of the diversity—in genre, subject, style, and experience—that Locke intended with *The New Negro* as a material register and mirror of African America in the second decade of the twentieth century.

A month earlier, the omnipresent W. E. B Du Bois, who contributed the essay "The Negro Mind Reaches Out" to Locke's volume, penned an important review for *Crisis*. As though forecasting *The New Negro*'s and the era's historical resonance, Du Bois opened with the contention that "this extraordinary book in many ways marks an epoch." Given his vantage point as editor of *Crisis*, Du Bois was well positioned to affirm and celebrate *The New Negro*'s unique place within a culture of print that focused increasingly on African America, as he did in noting that *The New Negro* "probably expresses better than any book that has been published in the last ten years the present state of thought and culture and it expresses so well and so adequately with such ramification into all phases of thought and attitude, that it is a singularly satisfying and inspiring thing."[19] This was no small claim on Du Bois's part.

Between 1915 and 1925, when *The New Negro* was published, a number of works by African American authors appeared in print, including Du Bois's own *Darkwater,* Marcus Garvey's *Philosophy and Opinions,* Georgia Douglas Johnson's *Heart of a Woman,* James Weldon Johnson's *Book of American Negro Poetry,* Claude McKay's *Harlem Shadows,* and Jean Toomer's *Cane*.[20] Pointing to its multifunctionality, Du Bois summarized Locke's vision for a standalone volume that would achieve greater permanence for a moment when black writers, as artistic pioneers, were influencing society and culture. With historical and sociological frames and displays of African Americans' cultural gifts across a number of genres distinguishing it from its predecessors, *The New Negro* also read as an archive that chronicled African American life and arts *interracially*. Containing essays from well-known writers both black and white, the volume also featured "Book Decorations" and "Drawings and Decorative Designs," mimeographs, and photographic reprints, along with fiction, poetry, drama, and a bibliography.

Du Bois judged *The New Negro,* as an anthology, to be "beyond criticism," asserting, "Mr. Locke has done a fine piece of editing."[21] Notwithstanding, with his review Du Bois appended to his praise for *The New Negro*'s malleability, and by implication its canonicity, the first of many criticisms that the volume accrued.[22] In a now famous critique, Du Bois wrote: "With one point alone do I differ with the Editor. Mr. Locke has newly been seized with the idea that Beauty rather than Propaganda should be the object of Negro literature and art. His book proves the falseness of his thesis." Again, writing from the perspective that *The New Negro* was a watershed moment, and therefore contending with Locke's ascendance as a pivotal arbiter of African American life and culture, Du Bois nevertheless took exception with Locke's insistence on "beauty" over "propaganda," lest "Mr. Locke's thesis . . . turn the Negro renaissance into decadence."[23] Despite his efforts, many of Du Bois's (and Locke's) contemporaries believed that such "decadence" limited the political viability of the period's arts.

The irony that Du Bois pointedly addressed in this review—the contrast between Locke's stated goals and what *The New Negro,* in Du Bois's reading, actually did—is related to another irony inscribing its multivalence. Whereas figures such as Du Bois criticized *The New Negro* for abandoning or minimizing the practice of defining and anthologizing African American life and culture for its historical and sociological value, others saw reflected in the volume too little of the artistic autonomy that Locke's invocation of aesthetic quality intimated was necessary to achieve this controversial beauty. Likely providing evidence for Du Bois's charge, Locke underscored his own hope for a future when it would be "no longer true that the Negro mind is too engulfed in its own social dilemmas for control of the necessary perspective of art."[24] Some writers argued that Locke's selection of poems, fiction, and essays for *The New Negro* as signs of a new consciousness and instances of artistic mastery emanating from throughout African America belied that very aim. Claude McKay, who was angry with Locke for changing the title of his poem "White House" to "White Houses," offered a pointed complaint in this regard, declaring that he "couldn't imagine such a man as the leader of a renaissance, [especially] when his outlook was so reactionary."[25] Other writers observed that *The New Negro* was a compendium of contradiction—claiming to display African America life at the confluence of new freedoms while constraining the very artists it lauded as proof of those freedoms.

Anthologizing Artists beyond *The New Negro*

As symbols of the "racial body," Harlem Renaissance literary anthologies presented and framed a writer's contributions as (part of) her developing corpus. Their featured writers embodied not simply the voices and perspectives of African America but the most innovative and potentially transformative of those voices and perspectives. For its readers, *The New Negro* was an invitation to witness and engage in a transformation of American life. Locke's own contributions to *The New Negro*—a foreword, his period-defining essay "The New Negro," and "Negro Youth Speaks"—operated as a dynamic and extended overview in this regard. With each instance of this framing narrative, Locke introduced, guided, persuaded, nurtured, and cultivated his readers. One read and could not help but become a version of Locke's New Negro reader. Locke's rhetorical style mirrored his work with emerging writers, who were *The New Negro*'s focus and achieved in it some two hundred pages of visibility. The volume promoted Du Bois, Braithwaite, and Fauset as recognizable names, enhanced the newfound celebrity of several of its younger contributors, and channeled the buzz from its earlier incarnation as a *Survey Graphic* special issue into greater prominence for Harlem Renaissance writers.

A few of Locke's contemporaries recognized and reenvisioned the model his anthology offered with their own compilations. Harlem Renaissance literary anthologies that appeared after *The New Negro* reflected their editors' desires to frame and introduce their compilations of African American literature as an appeal to readers to consider the writers therein artists. They openly sought to influence and even redefine readers' motivation for engaging the work of black writers. In ways similar to individual works of poetry and fiction, anthologies of African American literature recognized and negotiated the tastes and perspectives of the American reading public. As I discussed in chapter 1, oftentimes the framing of these volumes reflected editors' understanding of the difficulties that this readership presented to efforts to display the artistry that, for example, James Weldon Johnson documented in *The Book of American Negro Poetry*. The "finesse" that Horne attributed to that volume also enabled Johnson to address African American readers in particular, as his famed preface intimated that they, too, faced limitations in aiding a cohort of emerging writers grow a literary tradition. His 1931 article "The Dilemma of the Negro Author" made their roles in this regard explicit. Johnson argued that the African American writer had "no more absolute freedom to speak as he pleases addressing white America than he has in addressing black America."[26]

In the years following publication of *The Book of American Negro Poetry*, African American readers, especially middle-class arbiters of racial progress, expected literary representations that depicted African America as cultured and patriotic. With this burden of representation to negotiate, Johnson and his contemporaries claimed and argued for artistic autonomy in their efforts to reconcile as racial uplift their individual visions over more prescriptive efforts to produce so-called representative images. What Locke attempted in offering *The New Negro* as a balance between these perspectives served as a model for editors of subsequent anthologies in their efforts to advocate such autonomy and render it a benefit for African American readers. I turn now to a discussion of three of those successor anthologies: *Ebony and Topaz, Caroling Dusk,* and *Readings from Negro Authors*.

Ebony and Topaz

Even a cursory review of the contents of Charles Johnson's *Ebony and Topaz* reveals the impact of *The New Negro*. Of the three post–*New Negro* anthologies, *Ebony and Topaz, Caroling Dusk,* and *Readings from Negro Authors,* Johnson's volume was its most direct descendant. As editor of the National Urban League's magazine *Opportunity,* Johnson was particularly interested in blazing a different path with *Ebony and Topaz*. To do so, he introduced his volume with boldness and broke with convention. Johnson rejected the expectation for works by and about African Americans to function as a compendium of racial uplift. He wanted his readers to understand that "the most that will be claimed for this collection is that it is a fairly faithful reflection of current interests and observations in Negro life."[27] Although Johnson was not "usually given to personal, mean-spirited remarks about others," as his biographer writes, it is difficult not to read *Ebony and Topaz* as Johnson's challenge to *The New Negro*'s expressed interest in racial uplift.[28] His aims for *Ebony and Topaz* implicated *The New Negro* as capitulating to the demands of an audience that desired only racially affirming middle-class projections of African American life.

Given the editors' collaborative work in advancing the Harlem Renaissance and offering contributions to one another's volumes, Johnson's rejoinder—"This volume, strangely enough, does not set forth to prove a thesis nor plead a cause, nor, stranger still, to offer a progress report on the state of Negro letters"—was presumably more a response to the politics of racial representation than to Locke himself for conforming to it.[29] Nevertheless, his volume reads like a sequel to *The New Negro*'s concentration "upon self-expression and the forces and motives of self-determination," especially with its similar panoply of literary genres and racial images, and its own "Who's Who."[30] *Ebony and Topaz* revised Locke's volume, but not before reiterating its focus in two primary ways: practicing interracial collaboration and celebrating black folk life.

In *The New Negro,* Locke advanced the idea that "each generation . . . will have its creed." The contributors to *The New Negro,* he argued, affirmed the "efficacy of collective effort in race co-operation."[31] For example, a host of white American and European figures, including Nancy Cunard, Joel Spingarn, and Carl Van Vechten, worked with Du Bois, Georgia Douglas Johnson, and Wallace Thurman to cultivate black writers and promote their work as embodying New Negro ideology. Although African Americans' contributions dominated in both volumes, each editor enlisted the support of white counterparts such as Winold Reiss and Melville Herskovitz in *The New Negro* and Dorothy Scarborough and Ellsworth Faris in *Ebony and Topaz*. This interracial scope underscored the mission of pivotal racial uplift organizations such as the National Urban League to "improve the relations between the races."[32]

Additionally, when Locke's "Negro Youth" spoke, they were able to do so because they "[dug] deep into the racy peasant undersoil of the race life." Locke suggested that African Americans' folk culture was a rich landscape, which *The New Negro*'s writers tilled. He valued it as an artistic inspiration worthy of "alignment with contemporary artistic thought, mood, and style."[33] Whereas Locke invoked folk art as a medium for black artists to depart from, Johnson argued for it as a site of return, writing, "There is here [in black folk life] a life full of strong colors, of passion, deep and fierce, of struggle, disillusion—the whole gamut of life free from the wrappings of intricate sophistication."[34] With its sketches of black subjects from across the spectrum of African American life in Birmingham, Alabama, Nathan B. Young's "Eighteenth Street: An Anthology in Color" typified the tapestry that Johnson described. In offering representations of the folk as African America's modern subject, *Ebony and Topaz* chronicled how "the return of the Negro writers to folk materials proved a new emancipation."[35]

Through this distinction, *Ebony and Topaz* recast Locke's interest in the Harlem Renaissance vogue as a pointed demand for artistic freedom. In doing so, Johnson brought the promise of African American writers into sharper focus. Presenting *Ebony and Topaz* as "A Collectanea" did not immediately register Johnson's concerns with either authorship or readership. Whereas Locke's claim, in his framing essay "The New Negro," that "immediate hope [for rehabilitation of African American stereotypes] rests in the revaluation by white and black alike" only hinted at the biases of his targeted audience, Johnson anticipated bias explicitly in his introduction.[36] *Ebony and Topaz* was "a venture in expression," Johnson wrote, "shared with the slightest editorial suggestion by a number of persons who are much less interested in their audience than in what they are trying to say, and the life that they are trying to portray."[37] Among those "persons" was Langston Hughes, who had gained considerable notoriety since his work appeared in *The New Negro*. With Hughes's 1926 essay "The Negro Artist and the Racial Mountain" serving as a precursor and heralding Johnson's sentiment, *Ebony and Topaz* broadened the way racial uplift and racial pride functioned as "central preoccupations" and "controlling metaphors" in the discourse of the New Negro era.[38]

"The Negro Artist and the Racial Mountain" was an important manifesto for black writers who supported the notion that literature should be a tool for representing African American life in its fullness. In this response to George S. Schuyler's "Negro Art Hokum," Hughes argued that "the Negro artist works against an undertow of sharp criticism and misunderstanding from his own group and unintentional bribes from the whites. 'Oh, be respectable, write about nice people, show how good we are,' say the Negroes. 'Be stereotyped, don't go too far, don't shatter our illusions about you, don't amuse us too seriously. We will pay you,' say the whites." To those imposing this subversion and ultimate denial of the black artist's agency, Hughes pledged that "we younger Negro artists who create now intend to express our individual dark-skinned selves without fear or shame. If white people are pleased we are glad. If they are not, it doesn't matter. We know we are beautiful. And ugly too. The tom-tom cries and the tom-tom laughs. If colored people are pleased we are glad. If they are not, their displeasure doesn't matter either. We build our temples for tomorrow, strong as we know how, and we stand on top of the mountain, free within ourselves." In Hughes's reading, not only did a black literary tradition begin with the folk as "a great field of unused material," but also, if it was to thrive, it could not be constrained by desires for a literature that did not allow the individual artist to express her self and/or her race regardless of the views of others.[39]

Hughes conveyed these ideas in his poetry as well. His contribution to *Ebony and Topaz*, the poem "Dreamer," offered another perspective on the desire for unburdened creative expression. The unnamed speaker states:

> And I ask you:
> Do you understand my dreams?
> Sometimes you say you do
> And sometimes you say you don't.
> Either way
> It doesn't matter.
> I continue to dream.[40]

The "Dreamer" in Hughes's poem abandons his or her wish for a response from an unidentified "you" and continues to dream. "Dreamer" was the only piece by Hughes included in the anthology. Johnson probably chose to publish it because it described the shift that Johnson asserted black writers were then undergoing.

Johnson argued: "Negro writers, removed by two generations from slavery, are now much less self-conscious, less interested in proving that they are just like white people, and, in their excursions into the fields of letters and art, seem to care less about what black people think, or are likely to think about the race. Relief from the stifling consciousness of being a problem has brought a certain superiority to it."[41] Despite Du Bois's influential avowal that he did "not care a damn for any art that is not used for propaganda" resonating throughout African America and Johnson's own commitments to racial uplift, the *Opportunity* editor still framed *Ebony and Topaz* in such a way that African American readers compelled to dissent would recognize, if not accept, these New Negroes' demands for artistic freedom on their own terms.[42] As exemplified in Hughes's case, the relief that Johnson noted in his introduction to *Ebony and Topaz* came for young artists, to the extent that it did at all, only through their efforts to assert their authority and redefine the value and function of their literary art. Countee Cullen's *Caroling Dusk* was a tangible instance of this assertion.

Caroling Dusk

Acknowledging his readers' likely familiarity with the period's other literary anthologies, Countee Cullen opened his foreword to *Caroling Dusk* with the following observation: "It is now five years since James Weldon Johnson edited with a brilliant essay on 'The Negro's Creative Genius' *The Book of American Negro Poetry,* four years since the publication of Robert T. Kerlin's *Negro Poets and Their Poems,* and three years since from the Trinity College Press in Durham, North Carolina, came *An Anthology of Verse by American Negroes,* edited by Newman Ivey White and Walter Clinton Jackson." Identifying his reader as "the student of verse by American Negro poets," Cullen admitted that "there would be scant reason for the assembling and publication of another such collection were it not for the new voices that within the past three to five years have sung so significantly as to make imperative an anthology recording some snatches of

CHAPTER 3

their songs."[43] That Cullen did not list *The New Negro* among these other anthologies pointed to his reading of this tradition as an opportunity to return to a singular focus on poetry.

A celebrated poet in his own right, Cullen was in an ideal position to vet the "new voices" of African American literature. Through his column "The Dark Tower" for *Opportunity* magazine, which was often structured as a series of short reviews, Cullen praised and critiqued recently published materials. In June 1928, for example, he reviewed Leslie Pinckney Hill's *Toussaint L'Overture*:

> Design and research and a fine and sensitive appreciation of the uses of language all enter into the making and clothing of a pattern in the main highly successful. The foreword is an interesting document of open and candid intent: "I have also, in full view of all the risks, deliberately chosen blank verse as the only vehicle worthy of the dignity and elevation of my theme. We seem, as Mr. Trevelyan says, to have lost both taste and tradition for this high medium. Serious and sensitive writers must undertake to restore both. I can only hope that patient hospitality may be accorded to that measure and rhythm most expressive of the power and cadence of our tongue." That is an artistic presumption that we heartily applaud, confident that it emerges from a determination which does not hold that the use of blank verse is a strictly English monopoly, most un-American and distinctly un-Negro.[44]

Here Cullen praised Hill's choice of subject and form as much as what he perceived to be Hill's intention and identified approvingly with Hill's ability to speak through and about his own art.

Cullen's confidence in defining taste and tradition and encouraging this practice among his contemporaries linked this review to the project that was *Caroling Dusk*. As an extension of his perspectives on the work of young African American poets, *Caroling Dusk* carried on Cullen's efforts to position them as innovators and provocateurs. About Cullen's *Caroling Dusk* poets, *Crisis* contributor Idella Purnell noted, "With an unhappy heritage of poverty, prejudice, and contempt to combat, and with the happy heritage of ambitious minds, singing hearts, and a simple faith in ultimate goodness and justice, these carolers have the conflict and impetus necessary for the production of art."⁴⁵ Such a perspective shed light on Cullen's unique editorial practice. "The biographical notices carried with these poems," his foreword concluded, "have been written by the poets themselves . . . and if they do not reveal to a curious public all it might wish to know about the poets, they at least reveal all that the poets deem necessary and discreet for the public to know."⁴⁶

Affable, humorous, and with pointed sarcasm, Anne Spencer's autobiographical note typified Cullen's description. In it she revealed that she was "a Christian by intention, a Methodist by inheritance, and a Baptist by marriage." Spencer then turned to her craft: "I write about some of the things I love. But have no civilized articulation for the things I hate. I proudly love being a Negro woman—it's so involved and interesting. *We are the PROBLEM*—the great national game of TABOO."⁴⁷ Offering both criticism of the constraints of race pride and the "grueling race struggle" that James Weldon Johnson described in *The Book of American Negro Poetry,* and a not-so-veiled critique of the period's sexism through reference to Du Bois's millennial prediction about the "color line," Spencer's note exhibited more personality than those of most of her counterparts.⁴⁸ For her readers it had both endearing and off-putting potential. Regardless, it also afforded a glimpse of the woman behind the poems that followed and sounded the note of an artist entering the reader's consciousness on her own terms.

Claude McKay's account of his life's events presented another approach to these autobiographical notes. His readers learned that McKay, who published the period's defining poetry volume, *Harlem Shadows,* in 1922, was a "free-thinker." This early flexibility enabled him to read such "writers as Haeckel, Huxley, Matthew Arnold, side by side with Shakespeare and the great English novelists" before age fourteen.⁴⁹ In an instance of what Ben Glaser has described as "formal intertextuality,"⁵⁰ McKay aligned his literary influences and trajectory as a poet with an account of his travels—from Jamaica to the United States and to several cities in Europe, including, London, Berlin, and Paris—with the ways that he made a living. Passionately yet matter-of-factly, McKay recounted that he "went to work at various jobs, porter, houseman, longshoreman, barman, railroad club and hotel waiter. Kept on writing."⁵¹ Although McKay's presence in *Caroling Dusk* as an emerging but influential poet would matter to the "negro intelligentsia" that Locke's volume encouraged, McKay's biographical account served to connect with average black workers as well.[52] In offering such an account of his life, McKay affirmed and yet superseded Cullen's editorial aims. Through McKay's attention to his life as a laborer, *Caroling Dusk* spoke to the "porter, the barber, the maid, the teacher, [and] the handyman" as well.[53] The important gesture was that rather than have Cullen speak for him as editor, McKay spoke for himself as a worker and a poet.

In this and other ways, Cullen's *Caroling Dusk* went beyond *The New Negro* and its immediate contemporary, Johnson's *Ebony and Topaz*. Although both of those volumes promoted artistic freedom as a prerequisite for artistry, Cullen had another agenda, one to which Johnson merely alluded. Despite the criticisms that he faced—most famously Langston Hughes's veiled depiction of him in "The Negro Artist and the Racial Mountain"—Cullen asserted the right to produce art devoid of an intentionally racial focus.[54] This conception of artistic freedom circumscribed Cullen's contributions to the period. Whereas Johnson promoted *Ebony and Topaz* as a collection of works from more self-referential and ideologically independent black artists, with *Caroling Dusk* Cullen "sought to break with the racial tradition in poetry and, presumably, in other forms of expression."[55]

Kenneth Kinnamon has argued that "anthologies edited by famous writers often derive importance from what they reveal about the anthologist's literary tastes."[56] Cullen's extension of his literary oeuvre to the publication of *Caroling Dusk* demonstrated this pattern. Cullen presented *Caroling Dusk* as a framework for reading a collection of poems—"verse by Negro poets," as the anthology's subtitle noted—in which race was neither the central nor the most salient unifying characteristic. Clarifying his selection criteria in the volume's foreword, Cullen wrote, "While I do not feel that the work of these writers conforms to anything that can be called the Negro school of poetry, neither do I feel that their work is varied to the point of being sensational; rather is theirs a variety within a uniformity that is trying to maintain the higher traditions of English verse."[57] Cullen argued that the individual styles of African American poets of the period were informed less by race than by the poets' efforts to work within, master, and carry on celebrated poetic traditions. It was a claim that he evidenced through a brief overview of selected poets' themes.

He added in his foreword:

> A survey of the work of Negro poets will show that the individual diversifying ego transcends the synthesizing hue. From the roots of varied experiences have flowered the dialect of Dunbar, the recent sermon poems of James Weldon Johnson, and some of Helene Johnson's more colloquial verses, which, differing essentially only in a few expressions peculiar to Negro slang, are worthy counterparts of verses done by John V. A. Weaver "in American." Langston Hughes, poetizing the blues in his zeal to represent the Negro masses, and Sterling Brown, combining a similar interest in such poems as "Long Gone" and "The Odyssey of Big Boy" with a capacity for turning a neat sonnet according to the rules, represent differences as unique as those between Burns and Whitman. Jessie Fauset with Cornell University and training at the Sorbonne as her intellectual equipment surely justifies the very subjects and forms of her poems: "Touché," "La Vie C'est la Vie," "Noblesse Oblige," etc.; while Lewis Alexander, with no known degree from the University of Tokyo, is equally within the province of his creative prerogatives in composing Japanese *hokkus* and *tankas*.[58]

Cullen illustrated here the canonizing function of *Caroling Dusk,* demonstrating, for example, Hughes's and Brown's parity with Burns and Whitman.

Here and throughout the volume, *Caroling Dusk* revised the emerging anthological tradition, making mastery of forms and universality of theme the organizing principles. Through this approach Cullen responded to what he considered the sacrifice of good craft in favor of an explicitly racial focus, especially through dialect. He advocated this position in various venues and at times made it the basis of his criticism in "The Dark Tower." It was a position that provoked challenges. Several of his contemporaries responded to his appeals for mastery of craft as a rejection of black folk art in favor of European traditions. These critics read poems such as "Yet Do I Marvel"—with its concluding couplet: "Yet do I marvel at this curious thing / To make a poet black and bid him sing!"—as a reflection of Cullen's internalized racism.[59] Their perspectives structured an additional constraint against which Cullen wrote. In his preface Cullen engaged these tensions. *Caroling Dusk* continued a post-Locke editorializing that responded to and challenged audience expectations while it explicitly affirmed and created another autonomous space for Cullen and the poets featured in his volume.

Readings from Negro Authors

Compared with Johnson and Cullen, the editors of *Readings from Negro Authors* conveyed the viability of a literary anthology differently. In conceiving of and structuring a literary anthology as a textbook for schools and colleges, the editors went farther than did Johnson and Cullen, using the preface of their 1931 volume to argue what they would then go on to show: that Harlem Renaissance writers had various options for reaching America's reading publics. *Readings from Negro Authors* was an early effort to propel an investment in African American literature within educational institutions. The volume privileged poetry but contained other sections as well: "One-Act Plays," "Essays," and "Public Addresses." It concluded with "Biographical Sketches," a bibliography, and an important appendix which the editors titled "Suggestions for Study." These components positioned the contents of *Readings* as teachable, especially for the population of readers at African Americans institutions of higher learning.

As I illustrate further in chapter 4, schools and colleges were key settings for facilitating development of Harlem Renaissance literature. In his signal essay "Criteria for Negro Art," Du Bois celebrated the introduction of African American writers into classrooms across America, noting: "A professor in the University of Chicago read to a class that had studied literature, a passage of poetry and asked them to guess the author. They guessed a goodly company from Shelley and Robert Browning down to Tennyson and Masefield. The author was Countee Cullen."[60] *Readings* realized an important goal of the New Negro era and its Harlem Renaissance that Sterling Brown advocated: "the teaching of our youth that there is a great deal in our racial heritage of which we may be proud."[61] With appointments respectively in the English departments at Miner Teachers College and Fisk and Howard universities when they published *Readings*, the editors—Otelia Cromwell, Lorenzo Dow Turner, and Eva Beatrice Dykes—contributed a preface that paralleled Du Bois's introduction but, in this case, preparing a range of African American students for the racial pride and development of critical reading that *Readings* was designed to foster. From their experiences of working with their own students, the editors envisioned *Readings* as a means to reinterpret "the Progressive ideal of a more fully inclusive community and culture" and to understand "the problems and literary expressions of African Americans as inseparable from the problems and literary expressions of America."[62]

In a 1932 review of *Readings*, Mary Louise Strong echoed these ideas, arguing:

> Negro Literature is acquiring a history. It is developing critical tendencies. It has participated in several movements. It has made available wide ranges of material. It is making a valuable contribution. It is increasingly urgent in its demand for the Negro to conceive of a perfection in life and literature for higher than current levels and to dedicate himself anew to a quest of this higher perfection. The ultimate interpretation of American literature must be in terms of large issues of thought. Negro literature is the simple story of an oppressed and rising people. It is but one of the factors of the vast problem of American democracy and can be understood only in its organic relations to American literature and in the implications of American life. No one eager to understand American literature can afford to neglect this vital part. For that is not education which subordinates the quest for truth to the service of existing prejudice. It is high time that young America should begin this serious study. And here is an uncommonly opportune guide that shows how the task should be undertaken.[63]

The evidence for Strong's assertion first appears in the book's preface, where Cromwell, Turner, and Dykes imparted their shared editorial vision and noted: "The purpose of this volume is not to present another anthology of Negro literature, but to offer for classroom study or supplementary reading a selection of types of writings by Negro authors. Although many young people develop their reading habits independently of formal direction, teachers of English have a clear duty toward their students; namely, 'To teach them to read thoughtfully and with appreciation, to form in them a taste for good reading, and to teach them how to find books that are worthwhile.' "[64] The editors made it clear that their contribution to the genre of Harlem Renaissance literary anthologies was intended as much for teachers of literature as it was for students. In doing so they drew an explicit connection between their efforts and those of other educators such as Alice Dunbar-Nelson and Charles Eaton Burch, whose instructional goals centered on cultivating their students' critical reading and writing skills as a professional and ethical responsibility.[65] Even though Johnson and Cullen accepted limited editorial control in favor of artistic freedom and its potential to galvanize the literary tradition they celebrated, their volumes still participated in the complex work of defining who should represent any tradition, whether established or emerging, of African American letters.

The editors of *Readings* acknowledged their volume's bias in this regard. Attesting to the presence of a viable literary tradition but arguing that tradition should affirm only those works that were the best in quality and most appropriate in representation, they stated:

> In selecting material for this volume, the editors have been constrained to keep in mind their purpose, namely, the presentation of certain readings for definite study. No apology, therefore, is made for the offering of much that has appeared in print many times already or for the exclusion of writings that are of intrinsic worth yet not wholly suitable for textbook adoption. The particular slant of the realism of a few representative Negro writers and the marked predilection on the part of some others for a bafflingly incoherent style explain the absence from this volume of productions by one or two well-known writers.[66]

This note on editorial selection signaled the book's intended audiences and provoked reactions from those audiences. Perhaps because the editors expected the initial and hence most influential readers of their anthology to be skeptical but informed teachers of literature, they offered this statement to address potential charges of useless redundancy. In doing so, they answered the potential (and legitimate) question "Why should I use *Readings* when there are a number of collections of black literature available?"

Among the earliest African Americans to earn doctorates in English literature, Cromwell, Turner, and Dykes pointedly joined the debate among Harlem Renaissance writers about artistic freedom, especially the positions that Johnson and Cullen assumed, respectively, through *Ebony and Topaz* and *Caroling Dusk*.[67] In justifying their principles of exclusion as well as inclusion, Cromwell and her colleagues responded in advance to critics like Braithwaite, who, in reading Jean Toomer's *Cane* as a leading exemplar of the Harlem Renaissance, might have questioned its absence. (Although *Cane* is cited in their bibliography, the editors do not include an excerpt from it in the volume.) Indeed, what other critics defined as *Cane*'s experimental nature might well have been what Cromwell, Turner, and Dykes saw as a "particular slant of realism" and "marked predilection" unsuitable for their other group of intended readers: students.

Cromwell, Turner, and Dykes explicitly mediated their readers' relationships to the writers and works showcased in their volume. With their selections, the editors further demonstrated their belief that in order for younger generation writers to employ dialect, for example, or to feature the experiences of the poor or prostitutes through a blues lyric, there had to be an established body of work and conventions from which to depart. Because the editors offered *Readings* as an instance of African American writers' mastery of multiple forms without perpetuating racial stereotypes, the almost four-hundred-page anthology complemented the efforts to reshape the meaning of artistry that Locke's, Johnson's, and Cullen's volumes helped forge.

What *Readings* lacked in not offering unqualified support for artistic freedom it made up for as a tangible conduit for situating students and teachers as readers with the potential to recognize and appreciate artistry and do so critically. "Experience," the editors wrote, "has [also] shown that the plan of starting pupils with the writings of authors—*not* with what some one has said about the authors—is not only a logical procedure in the teaching of literature, but one calculated to challenge the imagination of the student."[68] Recalling the prefaces their predecessors had authored, this approach to reader orientation made the case for the special position of African American writers. For example, one of the volume's instructional units included several "love poems" to facilitate a reading of African American poetry as an artistic tradition. Cromwell, Turner, and Dykes started with a list of poems they felt represented African American poets' treatment of love as a theme, including Paul Laurence Dunbar, Angelina Weld Grimké, and Claude McKay.[69] Given this structure, students would begin their study with an introduction to a tradition of contemplating love, ranging from venerated African American poets such as Dunbar to rising stars of the Harlem Renaissance such as Georgia Douglas Johnson.

What followed the list of representative black poets was a series of prompts suggesting topics for the teacher and her students to explore. More than constituting a framework for "General Reading," as the subheadings noted, these prompts were also aimed at developing students' skill at close reading, analysis, and composition. *Readings* provided flexibility for a teacher to mount a study of "Negro authors" in poetry suited to the skills of her students. For example, a teacher might choose to have students locate and make use of evidence for their readings by instructing them, "As you read each poem, note its mood; then mark the passages that reveal specifically the mood." If the emphasis was on refining students' understanding of the use of language in the poems, the directive "Explain the word *blues* in the poem 'Play a Blues for Louise' " might have sufficed. To further their framework for studying the complexity of African American poetry and the versatility of the poets, the editors offered teachers and students an opportunity to consider the role of gender in poetic practices. In targeting skill development, the editors concluded with a prompt that asked students: "If you did not know anything of the authorship of these poems, do you think that you could tell which poems were written by men, and which by women? What would be your method of deciding about this feature of authorship?"[70]

Whether individually or collectively, just as they facilitated Cromwell, Turner, and Dykes's efforts to position African American poets and their works as worthy of rigorous study, the prompts provided throughout the "Suggestions for Study" did much to position "Negro authors" as viable subjects for nuanced literary instruction. The editors suggested, for example, that teachers have their students explain why "Poems Inspired by Nature" were classified as lyrics, or direct them to "make a study of three or four poems of each type of [Dunbar's] poetry," or ask them to "justify the verdict of the world or the feeling of the author" in exploring treatments of "The Poet."[71]

In addition, since the dual identification of African American literature that operated in *Readings* was both racial and nationalistic, it followed that in the "love poem" unit, the editors suggested that student readers "write a paragraph upon one of these subjects: 1. Sonnet XXI of *Sonnets from the Portuguese* and 'Dreamin' Town' [or] 2. 'Duncan Gray' and 'A Negro Love Song,' "[72] in other words, inviting them to explore the relationships between the poetry of Elizabeth Barrett Browning and Paul Laurence Dunbar in the former case and Robert Burns and Dunbar in the latter. Students' articulation of either question would depend on a number of dynamics such as those the editors noted in their preface. They structured *Readings* to anticipate students' (and teachers') interests in elements such as form, internal theme, or the poem's place within an American literary tradition, just a few of the suggested instructional frameworks. At these moments *Readings* not only demonstrated the use of Harlem Renaissance authors' modes of writing as an approach to literary study but also, as with historical and sociological explorations of black life and culture, rendered African American cultural arts as viable subject matter.[73]

Cromwell, Turner, and Dyke addressed students and teachers as specific segments of their audience and engaged with other educators' notions about the role that African American youth were to play in American society. Early in his career, Du Bois argued that educating African Americans was important as a way of developing "co-workers in the kingdom of culture."[74] Many creative writers and social critics understood the literature that the period's anthologies showcased as an investment in efforts

CHAPTER 3

to remake American society so that African Americans could enter into it and be a part of it more fully. Cromwell, Turner, and Dyke's contribution to the genre of Harlem Renaissance literary anthologies suggested just such a vision. In developing *Readings* specifically for use in America's educational institutions, both public and private, the editors attempted to actualize two goals of the Harlem Renaissance at once: stimulating racial pride and changing perceptions of African Americans in order to achieve social acceptance and equality.

In offering students an opportunity to respond to Alain Locke's essay "Our Little Renaissance," which first appeared in Johnson's *Ebony and Topaz*, the authors asked an important question: "What is the significance of the term *Negro Renaissance?*"[75] The lack of extant student papers makes it impossible to know for certain, but those who responded to the prompt probably offered "some sort of critical appraisal," as Locke did, of the still emerging renaissance in letters among African Americans.[76] In an important way, *Readings* invited students to support the effort to make literary tradition as well. Even though its frameworks and conceptions of audience differed from those of other Harlem Renaissance literary anthologies, a drive to evoke a New Negro reading experience in order to achieve such cultural literacy can be felt throughout *Readings*. Like the editors of preceding and contemporaneous volumes, *Readings'* editors structured their anthology in such a way as to lead its audience to read literature and engage artistry dynamically.

As three literary anthologies meant to advance the cultural work of *The New Negro, Ebony and Topaz, Caroling Dusk,* and *Readings from Negro Authors* were representative of Harlem Renaissance literary anthologies that fused direct address to their readers with opportunities for active consideration of artistry. Some editors, like Johnson, signaled the purpose of their volume by deemphasizing racial uplift in favor of racial pride predicated on artistic independence. Others, especially writer-anthologists like Cullen, made literature a central focus without explicit context and only on the writer's terms. These practices further reveal the shape and nature of the dialogue that existed between Harlem Renaissance writers and their readers.

The precedent of anthologizing to enable a reader's tangible experience with innovative and racially influential poetry and fiction operated similarly to projections of the New Negro. Just as the latter effected neither an immediate change in race relations nor wholesale racial pride, the appeals for and support of black writers' artistry and independence through the former did not eliminate the need for deliberate editorial practices and frameworks. Although targeting a more specific audience of readers presented *Readings from Negro Authors* with challenges different from those facing *Ebony and Topaz* or *Caroling Dusk,* its editors' claims about the imperative of their literary anthology as a mechanism for cultural display and exchange were no less explicit. Such explicit framing in later Harlem Renaissance literary anthologies demonstrated the existence of an African American literary tradition that was proving itself central to American literature more broadly. It also furthered the efforts of Harlem Renaissance writers at inviting a New Negro reader's engagement with a literary tradition based on artistic mastery and independence.

PEDAGOGY FOR CRITICAL READERSHIP

James Weldon Johnson's English 123

◆▸◆◂

In his autobiography *Along This Way,* James Weldon Johnson reflected on his appointment as the Adam K. Spence Professor of Creative Literature at Fisk University in the 1930s:

> I am almost amused at the eagerness with which I go to meet my classes. The pleasure of talking to them about the things that I have learned and the things that I have thought out for myself is supreme. And there is no less pleasure in drawing from them things that they have learned and the things that they have thought out for themselves. I realize that, though I am nominally the teacher, there are many new things that I shall be taught. In touch with the youth of my race in a great university of the South, I shall be zealous to learn what they are thinking, how the world looks to them, and what goals they are pressing toward. I feel that on this favorable ground I shall be able to help effectively in developing additional racial strength and fitness and in shaping fresh forces against bigotry and racial wrong.[1]

English 123, "The Negro in American Literature," the course that Johnson taught as part of his appointment, was an instance of the exchange that

Pedagogy for Critical Readership

he expected. In teaching the "youth of [his] race," Johnson promoted a New Negro reader in a forum beyond his writings while sustaining such advocacy through face-to-face interaction with actual readers.

As Johnson's reminiscence suggests, African American youth had a presence in virtually every facet of life in early-twentieth-century America. The students Johnson taught were among the youth aged fifteen to nineteen years old who made up almost 11 percent of the African American population in 1930.[2] In the years following the 1929 stock market crash, some members of this younger generation who were students at Fisk struggled to keep up their morale and their tuition payments. As Joe Richardson has documented: "Enrollment [at Fisk] dropped from 439 in 1930 to 317 in 1934. In December 1932, students owed the university over $7,000 in tuition for the first semester. Thirty pupils left school the same year for financial reasons. Of the 141 students who failed to return between 1934 and 1936, approximately 40 gave financial difficulty as their reason and 31 others transferred to cheaper schools." These dynamics suggest that students had to address practical concerns as well as meet the academic demands of Fisk's curriculum. These practical concerns also appear to have included national and world problems. In 1933 the lynching of Cordie Cheek, a local black resident who was abducted near the Fisk campus, concerned the students greatly and prompted a series of protests. The most pointed one occurred in 1934. When President Franklin Roosevelt "visited the campus to hear the Fisk Choir sing one of his favorite spirituals—'Ain't Gonna Study War No More'—he was handed a petition signed by 250 students protesting the Scottsboro case in Alabama, the lynching of Claude Neal at Marianna, Florida, and violence in general."[3]

Considered alongside Johnson's expectations of what teaching Fisk students would entail and how he would identify with them, this institutional context resonates with Christine Pawley's suggestion that how historical readers are imagined "should in principle have something to do with how readers imagined themselves."[4] As I show in what follows, Johnson's handwritten notes for English 123 contain indicators of the way he responded to such self-imagining on the part of his students. More explicitly stated was Johnson's intention to develop his students' study of literature as a complement to Fisk's focus on African American life and culture. A merger of Johnson's own poetry, fiction, essays, music, and notions about history, the American literary canon, and the aesthetics of African American arts, his English 123 was structured as a nine-part lecture series aimed at making the case for an African American literary tradition. Johnson afforded his students the opportunity for detailed and sustained consideration of how he read—and, by implication, how they might read—this literary tradition. In this respect English 123 was also a compelling venue for addressing, if not solving, the problems of readership that Johnson contemplated throughout his career.

Johnson's Early Criticism

According to Richard Carroll, Johnson was an atypical but influential literary critic who was "primarily concerned with the black writer—what he needs to know, and what he must do in order to produce his best work."[5] These concerns were central to *The Book of American Negro Poetry*. For example, in the preface Johnson articulated one particular problem facing Harlem Renaissance writers: "I know the question naturally arises . . . why have not the millions of Negroes in the United States with all the emotional and artistic endowment claimed for them produced a Dumas, or a Coleridge-Taylor, or a Pushkin?" Johnson suggested that these were legitimate comparisons and acknowledged his readers' likely questions, urging them to accept as an answer his belief that "the Negro in the United States is consuming all of his intellectual energy in this grueling race-struggle."[6] Johnson also responded to some critics' "reservations about writing by black Americans,"[7] pointing to recent achievements in African American poetry as a rapid development that should motivate people to discard what he considered increasingly dated notions of African Americans' creative contributions.

While racial uplift was an initial goal, and remained a necessary one for African Americans' literary output throughout the period, for Johnson the time had come for a purpose beyond racial uplift alone. He identified that purpose in his preface as the development of an African American artistry able to construct a form "expressing the imagery, the idioms, the peculiar turns of thought, and the distinctive humor and pathos, too, of the Negro, but which will also be capable of voicing the deepest and highest emotions and aspirations, and allow of the widest range of subjects and the widest scope of treatment." Johnson saw great potential in poetry as a precursor to this aesthetic yet still intangible form and noted throughout the volume's selections early and contemporaneous indicators of its development in the works of writers such as Claude McKay and Anne Spencer. Johnson also understood that in order for the "colored poet in the United States" to do "what Synge did for the Irish," more was needed than a new literary form.[8]

Specifically, "the colored poet" also needed an informed audience, a requirement that Johnson acknowledged in his preface and attempted to cultivate. He envisioned a more constructive reader-writer relationship that would recognize as a first step "the undeniable creative genius of the Negro."[9] Johnson's preface did not simply introduce his *Book of American Negro Poetry*. When read in context, his arguments also framed and established a precedent for his later efforts to address and resolve the problems endemic to the relationship between African American writers and their reading publics. An explicit instance of this cultural work is Johnson's essay "The Dilemma of the Negro Author."

Whereas, in his preface to *The Book of American Negro Poetry*, Johnson wrote about and to a general American public as his literary audience, in this 1928 article in the *American Mercury*, Johnson went further in describing that audience explicitly as both black and white. "The Aframerican author faces a special problem," he wrote, "which the plain American author knows nothing about—the problem of the double audience. It is more than a double audience; it is a divided audience, an audience made up of two elements with differing and often opposite and antagonistic points of view. His audience is always both white America and black America."[10] Johnson underscored the layers of segregation that informed notions of race in early-twentieth-century America, then rhetorically united African American writers' dual audience while acknowledging their differing needs and expectations. Just as he did in the preface to *The Book of American Negro Poetry*, in "The Dilemma" Johnson wrote explicitly to and about the white readers (embodied in *American*

Mercury's predominant audience) who also fueled the Harlem Renaissance.

Identifying the problem more concretely as a perpetual challenge for the black writer in deciding "to whom he shall address himself," Johnson charged this readership with creating and maintaining "many longstanding artistic conceptions about the Negro" and "a whole row of hardest stereotypes which are not easily broken up."[11] From the archetypal caricatures of the ignorant darkie, coon, and mammy of slavery, to the perception, fueled by the realities of internal migration, of African Americans as immoral vagrants and the cause of urban blight, African Americans encountered a barrage of stereotypes and related policies that served to perpetuate notions of black inferiority, depravity, and inhumanity. Like other Harlem Renaissance writers, Johnson made countering these images and practices central goals of his contributions to the print and visual cultures that portrayed African American life.

In painting a fuller picture of the black writer's dilemma, Johnson also argued that the expectations of African Americans were often shaped by a "defensive state of mind" as they read works depicting their experiences. He provided this scenario as an illustration: "It is quite possible for a Negro author to do a piece of work, good from every literary point of view, and at the same time bring down on his head the wrath of the entire colored pulpit and press, and gain among the literate element of his own people the reputation of being the prostitutor of his talent and a betrayer of his race—not by any means a pleasant position to get into."[12] Here Johnson identified the African American press and religious community as crucial barometers of African American public opinion at the time. He pointed specifically to the backlash that both generated and then functioned as the discourse that Sterling Brown later described as "supersensitive criticism."[13]

Given that he was an accomplished and respected member of the older generation of Harlem Renaissance writers, Johnson presumably managed the dilemma somewhat better than his younger contemporaries. Removed in time from "some doubters" among the reviewers of *Autobiography of an Ex-Coloured Man* when it had premiered in 1912, by 1928 Johnson could draw on years' worth of his own experiences to articulate the challenges of the black writer's double audience.[14] With reflections and commentaries such as "The Dilemma," Johnson turned his attention to an advocacy poised to benefit the period's younger and, in some instances, more independent writers such as Langston Hughes, Zora Neale Hurston, Richard Bruce Nugent, and Wallace Thurman, whose own encounters with this dilemma led them in part to conceive and publish the journal *FIRE!!* in 1926.

In concluding "The Dilemma," Johnson envisioned a time when "there will come a breaking up and remodeling of most of white America's traditional stereotypes" and when "Black America will abolish many of its taboos."[15] Measured in his hopefulness, Johnson suggested that such changes were prerequisites for unifying this double audience and enabling fuller expression of black artists' autonomy. One of several commentaries to complement the increased publication and reception of Harlem Renaissance writers' works, "The Dilemma of the Negro Author" did not pose concrete solutions to the problems that Johnson described. Instead, it further developed his criticism and treated writers' concerns about their readers as viable topics for the public exchanges about African American literature occurring in the press, in schools and colleges, at club meetings, and among Harlem Renaissance writers themselves. With English 123, "The Negro in American Literature," Johnson turned his criticism into pedagogy and structured a course to bring about the kinds of changes that he called for in "The Dilemma."

Teaching in the New Negro Era

Johnson's political, artistic, and critical oeuvre exhibited the integrated approach to advancing African American life and culture that he had demonstrated earlier during his tenure at the Stanton School in Jacksonville, Florida, and then applied in his work at Fisk University. When Johnson accepted the position of principal at Stanton in 1894, it was a grade school, the largest public school for African Americans in Florida. By 1896 he had expanded it into the first public high school for blacks in the state. Understanding the benefits of pre-collegiate training in a high school curriculum, Johnson devised a plan to educate students so they

CHAPTER 4

would not only graduate but also be prepared to attend college.

As he recounted in *Along This Way*:

> I first got the members of the class interested in the project; then I persuaded their parents to let them come back the following year. I laid out a course for them that was practically the Junior Prep course at Atlanta University. I myself taught the class. The next year I followed the same procedure, told the superintendent what I had done, and asked for an assistant. I discontinued the use of the general assembly room for devotions and converted it, by using curtains for partitions, into extra classrooms. The next year I obtained another assistant. I introduced Spanish as the modern language course and taught it myself. That, in short, is the plan by which Stanton Grade School was developed into Stanton High School.[16]

Not surprisingly, Johnson's work with African American youth in Jacksonville's public schools also facilitated his goal for the song that became the "Negro National Anthem": "Lift Every Voice and Sing."

After its first public performance, "the schoolchildren of Jacksonville kept singing it; some of them became schoolteachers and taught it to their pupils. Within twenty years the song was being sung in the schools and churches and on special occasions throughout the South and in some other parts of the country."[17] Although Johnson and his brother Rosamond wrote the lyrics and the score, it was subsequent generations of students and teachers who turned the song into the sign of racial pride and progress that it became. In this and other ways, Johnson shaped African Americans' education into a site for fostering intellectual rigor and racial pride. This work informed his critical treatment of literature and was welcomed at a changing Fisk.

Once the "rage for Harlem" faded by the 1930s and white patron interest in African Americans' cultural arts diminished, Fisk University became "a final captive for the Renaissance."[18] While Fisk had flourished financially under president Fayette A. McKenzie (1915–1925), who secured the institution's first million-dollar endowment, it also experienced a great degree of internal and external turmoil. McKenzie was an authoritarian at Fisk and was sympathetic to the interests of industrial philanthropists, who supported his admonitions to the students to "eschew political and social questions and concentrate on interracial cooperation and economic development."[19] When Thomas Elsa Jones assumed the presidency in 1926, after "students were able to depose 'the dictator' and restore the silenced newspaper," he had the arduous task of moving Fisk forward and gaining the support of students, alumni, faculty, and benefactors.[20] He fostered a period of momentum that included not just the university's various constituencies but the surrounding Nashville community as well. A central element of Jones's efforts involved recruiting for its faculty men and women who were well trained in academic disciplines and who could represent the interests of African America. Fortunately for Jones, the generation of African Americans born just after the end of slavery was ready to lead.

Having met James Weldon Johnson at a race relations conference a few years earlier, Jones recruited him to teach at Fisk just as Johnson was completing a leave of absence from the NAACP. Jones was thinking, he told Johnson, of creating a position at Fisk "analogous to that held by Robert Frost at Amherst College."[21] Johnson's presence on the Nashville campus, along with that of sociologist E. Franklin Frazier, literary scholar Lorenzo Dow Turner, and archivist Arna Bontemps, would make Fisk a center in the study of social science and African American cultural arts.

Beginning with Jones's leadership, and continuing throughout Charles S. Johnson's tenure as its first African American president, Fisk University "encouraged integration both racially and through the inclusion of a broader range of experiences within the college curriculum." Charles Johnson "built a campus in which English majors attended art exhibitions, students in the sciences attended lectures on colonial imperialism, and sociology majors screened foreign and avant-garde film. And in doing so, he created an environment that nurtured future intellectuals and leaders among the African American community."[22]

On English 123

Although it was historic because of James Weldon Johnson's influence, its comprehensive scope, and the endowed professorship that enabled it, English 123 was not the first documented literature course to feature the work of African American writers. For example, Charles Eaton Burch, a contemporary of Johnson's and a professor of English at Howard University, taught a course called "Poetry and Prose of Negro Life."[23] In his 1921 article "Freshman Papers in a Negro College," Burch reported to *Crisis* readers that his students "again and again turn to the Negro world" as content for and a topical source of their writing. He sensed "the sad cry of despair and the confident notes of hope" in these student texts, which attempted to "reach out and speak to America and sometimes the British Empire."[24]

Burch clearly understood the realities of student life beyond the classroom, especially the desires of young people for social advancement. Through his characterization of them in *Crisis*, Burch positioned his students as emerging critical readers and writers who detailed the social injustices that African Americans faced. Burch conceived of the "work of expression" in this first-year composition course "as an opportunity for generating democratic community, not primarily through a standardization of diction, but through shared exposition of a familiar experience."[25]

Along with Burch and a host of other educators, including Sterling Brown, Otelia Cromwell, Eva Beatrice Dykes, Alice Dunbar Nelson, and Lorenzo Dow Turner, James Weldon Johnson was an early contributor to curricular advances that positioned African American literature as a primary tool of instruction in formal education. His belief that the study of African American literature required a diverse body of works, an understanding of African American cultural traditions, and an examination of African American artistry were the conceptual sites through which he introduced "The Negro in American Literature" to his Fisk students.

Among Johnson's archived papers at Yale University's Beinecke Rare Book and Manuscript Library are a series of handwritten lecture notes, typed and handwritten versions of a course description, and a typed bibliography for English 123. Although the handwritten lecture notes addressing themes such as "African art—its Influence," "the passing of dialect," and "the rise of American Negro prose" lack specific dates, Johnson likely used them as early as spring 1933, the semester referred to in the course description.[26] Given the formality of diction and the list of paper topics that his students pursued, it is probable that Johnson prepared this course description to outline the focus, structure, and student work for an audience beyond the course.

English 123, Johnson noted, "is a study of the Negro in American Literature. It considers him both as literary material and also as a writer. The use of the Negro character by white writers is followed chronologically from the early humorous or pathetic treatment to the varied and complex character portrayals of the present day. The development of the simple folk character into the highly integrated individual surrounded by complicated circumstances is studied in detail."[27] The outline signaled the value that Johnson accorded to studying literary representations of African Americans as a chronicle of the influence of African American writers and artists. It also reflected the Harlem Renaissance's emphasis on the "present day" and the transformative potential of its artists to craft more authentic representations of African Americans' humanity.

Johnson's "Inaugural Lecture" echoed this description and clarified the structure and significance of the course. His outline, which opened with the heading "Negro Literature," engaged "two points of view" for studying "American Negro Literature." "Lecture 2," which built on the first, considered "Negro life and characters" as the subject of much creative writing—poetry, fiction, and drama—especially in the works of white American authors. "Lecture 3" addressed "Negro poets." "Lecture 4" continued Johnson's preceding focus on African American poetic traditions. "Lecture 5" illustrated what Johnson called a "sublimation of dialect." "Lecture 6" compared African Americans' efforts in poetry to their mastery of prose. "Lecture 7" addressed influential writers of prose such as Chesnutt and Du Bois.[28]

Johnson's notes for his "Mandate Lecture," or eighth lecture, indicated that it was "the last of [his] lectures in the course," and was so named because it bowed to his students' request that he offer "a brief survey of Negro American poets" and read "some of [his] own poems, and [comment] a little on [his] own creative processes."[29] Johnson's "Creative Genius Lecture" is the most difficult of the units to place sequentially, but it included as one component of its focus Johnson's assertion that "America would not be precisely the America it is except for the influences brought to bear [by African Americans] in its making."[30] This set of notes constitutes a rich tapestry of ideas and insightful illustrations of the confluence of Johnson's multiple roles throughout the New Negro era and its Harlem Renaissance.

Despite his concerns about the limitations of African American readership and the multiple efforts to cultivate it, Johnson's criticism lacked an explicit argument about how formal teaching generally, and English 123 in particular, might function as a way to develop readers. Therefore I examine these records of his teaching for evidence of Johnson's own cultural literacy and the literacy he wished to shape for his students. English 123, I contend, provides much insight into how Johnson targeted this segment of the Harlem Renaissance's younger generation as having the potential to become New Negro readers "strong enough to render a constantly sensitive and defensive attitude on the part of the race unnecessary and distasteful."[31]

In keeping with the myriad ways in which he and other creative writers and critics modeled approaches for a New Negro reader through their commentaries, the lecture notes for English 123 further detailed Johnson's critical and culturally informed reading practices. For example, framed through personal observations, his "Inaugural Lecture" contrasted with the formality of the course description. Johnson clarified his instructional goals for his students throughout this ten-page text and wrote himself into the discussion as a different type of scholar-artist. As the introduction to the series, Johnson's "Inaugural Lecture" brought Fisk students into dialogue with the contextual dynamics that shaped the subject of the series. "Ladies and Gentlemen," he opened. "Let me say in beginning that in these talks I am to give I shall make a special effort to be non-academic in the manner of expressing myself. I shall try to avoid as far as I am able the [illegible] and stereotypes of literary criticism and to stick as closely as I can to universal English."[32]

When, in the late 1920s, scholars devised terminology and an approach for studying American literature aimed at fostering intellectual rigor, the teaching of that subject underwent important methodological and conceptual changes.[33] While Johnson did not offer an explanation for opening with this disclaimer, even at this stage in American education, he may have felt the need to dispel students' concerns that the content of his lecture series might be too formal and abstract. In analyzing Johnson's criticism, Richard Carroll gave impetus to such a suggestion when he argued: "Johnson does not spend his energies discussing the abstract questions of aesthetic theory which have traditionally been of interest to literary critics. Such concerns as defining and describing the nature of poetry, the power of imagination, and the relation of form to content, for example, he passes over lightly."[34] While a number of motivating factors are plausible, I read Johnson's desire to position himself (and his lectures) outside a received tradition of American literature and in an accessible language as a moment when Johnson's oratory and his critical agenda converge. Whatever his specific motivation, given the way he remembered his role at Fisk in *Along This Way,* Johnson's self-positioning in his "Inaugural Lecture" clearly reflected a desire to connect with his students.

After this clarification and initial effort to reach out, Johnson succinctly outlined the content of his "talks." He wrote: "We are to discuss the general subject of the Negro in American Literature. We shall divide the subject roughly into the following three divisions: 1. The Negro as a subject or character in Am. Lit. The Negro in Am. Lit. as a creator. 2. Some limitations on Negro writers. 3. Under the heading of the Creative Genius of the Negro—we shall in a general way discuss the artistic creative powers of the Negro, both potential and demonstrated. This is the way I have planned it."[35] This additional outline reflected the method and terms that Johnson employed in presenting *The Book of American Negro Poetry.* As this plan suggests, Johnson structured a specialized literary history, consideration of the black writer, and examination of African American cultural production as useful ways to engage students in studying American literature.

The typography of his "Inaugural Lecture" becomes significant in this regard. From Johnson's annotations to this outline it appears that he had initially intended to present the first of his three "divisions" as two separate points. Combining the two units instead and juxtaposing "the Negro as subject" with "the Negro as creator" allowed him to demonstrate the importance of the recent renaissance in letters for revising the treatment of African Americans in American literature. His change can be read as practical in yet another way: a discussion of the Harlem Renaissance as a site of innovation would make an appropriate frame for his thoughts on African American writers. A key implication of these changes and the lecture series title has to do with Johnson's pointed categorization of the African American literary tradition as *American*. With this (re)framing, Johnson extended his advocacy of a long-held perspective about African American citizenship, one that other figures articulated as well throughout New Negro era. Johnson's efforts to explain this perspective across his writings inspired his readers to view African Americans' literary contributions as an essential part of American literature. A reconception of American literature and a claim of ownership, Johnson's lectures advanced Fisk's work of building students' shared sense of both racial and national pride.

Johnson also positioned English 123 as a context for addressing contemporary racial dilemmas in 1930s America. We see this in his references to the obvious limitations of his course. He wrote in his notes for the "Inaugural Lecture": "I need not say that we have here laid out an area that cannot be adequately covered in 3 hours. Perhaps it could be done in 30 hours. For, contrary to the common notion, the amount of printed matter that is concerned in one way or another with the Negro is *enormous*. I venture to say that more pages have been written and printed on the Negro than upon any other single subject in America—with the possible exception of religion and social politics—and the Negro enters most of the discussion of social politics" (4–5).

Again drawing on what he defined as commonly accepted notions, Johnson sought to alter his students' perceptions of American literature. To students concerned about the dearth of materials pertaining to a study of African American life and culture, Johnson asserted that there was sufficient literature to justify an extensive course. Indeed for Johnson, such a course would merely be a beginning. There was much subject matter to cover, as his marginal note "Monroe Work—17,000 entries—the bulk of them re—American Negro" attested, a reference to Monroe Work's 1928 *Bibliography of the Negro in Africa and America*, cited in his notes along with other evidence for his claim. His concerns here built on his efforts to insert into American literary history a body of work on black life and culture. English 123 ensured that this oeuvre would be accessible in the context of African Americans' higher education.[36]

As a pragmatic response to the perceived difficulties in achieving such inclusion, Johnson's attention to the available resources for studying "the Negro in American literature" bridged the lecture series' apparent distance from Fisk University's focus on social science. Johnson noted that "in discussing the Negro in literature in particular and in art in general it might seem that we are departing from the scientific, factual, and actual aspects of the question which is the paramount one before the Institute of Race Relations—that we are passing over practically into the realm of the imagination. I am confident that the opposite is true" (6). By 1930, Fisk students were aware of the value of social science in addressing the status of black America for two reasons. The first and most obvious was Fisk's social science department, headed by Charles S. Johnson beginning in 1928. With courses such as Sociology 124, Fisk students had the opportunity to study "the social psychological backgrounds of Negro status in America, the evolution of social attitudes; the interplay of economics and social forces in successive patterns of race relations, with special emphasis upon problems of industry, agriculture, housing, crime, citizenship, and race relations."[37] Much of the material for this course came from faculty research and publications.[38]

The second reason had to do with what Kevin Gaines characterizes as a turn to an "academic sociological discourse of uplift" among African American leaders and scholars during the New Negro era.[39] Charles S. Johnson's work with the Institutes of Race Relations during the 1930s is one indicator of this turn. James Weldon Johnson was aware of these institutes, such as the one at Swarthmore College, where, in 1933, Charles Johnson brought together "social scientists and leaders of community action groups to study racial problems with a view toward taking practical measures to reduce racial tensions and further equality of opportunity,"[40] which he refers to in his "Inaugural Lecture." James Weldon Johnson's work as NAACP secretary and his related activism made him sympathetic to the institutes and the questions they raised. Johnson's investment in artistic expression, his own and that of African America, was also a manifestation of his efforts to advance social equality. Relating his lectures to the "race question" expressed Johnson's desire to position the study of literature and art as equally practical ways of achieving this goal.

CHAPTER 4

Mindful, then, of the increasing influence of a social science poised for political and social activism, particularly at Fisk, Johnson appears to have included these issues in order to address the possibility that English 123 would be viewed as incompatible with or irrelevant to an approach that other black leaders were advocating. "Literature and art," he wrote, "furnish not only a reflection, a synthesis, a summary of the actual social conditions and the communal modes of thought and action—I am almost tempted to say mores—but are conservators of those conditions and modes" (7). Like Alice Dunbar-Nelson, who argued in "Negro Literature for Negro Pupils" that "statistics mean nothing to children. The child mind must have concrete examples, for it is essentially poetic and deals in images. It is not enough to say that black men fought in the Revolutionary War to the extent of so many in so many regiments," Johnson positioned literature and art as complements to rather than competitors with social science.[41] Indeed, both Johnson and Dunbar-Nelson maintained that the study (and production) of literature had the potential to give substance to the facts of African American life that social scientists studied.

As a central focus of his "Inaugural Lecture," Johnson articulated at length his views on the viability of art in addressing African American social reality. "We should bear in mind," he clarified, "that the Negro has 2 sets of factors to contend against: those involved in actual conditions and those involved in stereotyped opinions. And these stereotypes are as real and difficult to deal with as the actual conditions" (7–8). While addressing part of a strategy for resolving the problems of black life, Johnson's English 123 reflected his effort to make students aware of how social science, literature, and literary study achieved similar goals. This effort was yet another way in which Johnson used his "Inaugural Lecture" to advocate long-held beliefs as conceptual and practical frames for studying "the Negro in American literature."

Johnson concluded his notes for the "Inaugural Lecture" with the following:

> In literature and art these stereotypes are given currency and are conserved. It is also true that by literature they are in a large measure modified, changed, and abolished. Literature and art

offer a technique that may be called the Art Approach to the Race question—and quite a feasible approach it is. It leads to a *level* platform on which, perhaps, more people—white and black[—]are willing to stand than upon any other. I feel that what the Negro himself has done in literature and art in the last two decades has greatly broadened that platform and gone far to break up many of the old stereotypes (9–10).

The Harlem Renaissance provided Johnson ample evidence for his reading of the importance of the "art approach." For him it was a success because African American writers had provoked interracial considerations of race by presenting images of black life that contrasted with those in received American literature and art.

Johnson and the Students of English 123

As a point of departure in charting Johnson's development of literary criticism aimed at cultivating a New Negro reader in the later years of the Harlem Renaissance, the lecture notes for English 123 demonstrate how Johnson planned to employ, intervene in, and (re)construct literary canons as well as historicize American literary traditions in terms of race. I also read them as important, if partial, instances of Johnson's own critical literacy practices and advocacy for such among his students. Three additional units of the series are instructive in this regard.

As the second part of "a hasty review of the Negro poets," "Lecture 4" presented Johnson's study of Paul Laurence Dunbar's life, his artistry, and the critical reception of his work. In his notes for this lecture Johnson wrote, "Dunbar's fame rests mainly on his Negro dialect poetry" (1). Johnson then complicated the basis of Dunbar's popularity. He suggested a process of consolidation, and pointed to the influence of entertainment media as an explanation for the limitations of Dunbar's dialect poems. "Dialect," he wrote, "[came] to him fixed, rigid, stereotyped. In the mould [sic] cast by the minstrel stage. If it had been otherwise, Dunbar might have done with Negro dialect what Burns did with Scottish dialect" (1). As a complement to the ideas he penned earlier, specifically in his first two lectures, about "how the Negro has been treated as a character" by white authors, and a

CHAPTER 4

lament for Dunbar's unrealized potential, Johnson reiterated his belief that dialect poetry and the social forces encouraging its production acted as constraints on African American writers' artistry. Critical of the way the subgenre was consumed throughout his career, here Johnson distinguished between the use of dialect for stereotype and its use to represent the spirit and corporeality of a people, emphasizing that Dunbar's artistry was too often associated with the former.

Johnson did not limit his efforts at contemplating popular understandings of Dunbar's poetry to this distinction and its implications. He affirmed Dunbar's complexity and versatility, repositioning him as a forerunner to post–World War I African American poets whose "motivation" was to voice "what the race was *then* experiencing" (2). Before mentioning poets such as Fenton Johnson and Georgia Douglas Johnson and guiding students to examples of their work in *The Book of American Negro Poetry* (Johnson included marginal page references for several of these poets, noting them in the following way: "McKay—a superb lyricist also *Flame Heart* Am. N. P. 174"), Johnson illustrated another measure of Dunbar's primacy (2).

As point "(c)" in his discussion of Dunbar, Johnson made this marginal notation: "The cry of the race in Dunbar's literary English poems— *not in his dialect*" (1). On an additional but unnumbered page of notes for "Lecture 4," Johnson listed several titles under the phrase "Dunbar's race conscious poems," including "To Ethiopia," an "early" poem, and the canonical "We Wear the Mask." Along with this list were references to pages where the poems appeared in *The Book of American Negro Poetry* and the phrase "contemplate passages," which he repeated with each title. Although vague, Johnson's phrase here possibly meant that he intended to have students read these "race conscious poems" and compare and contrast them with Dunbar's dialect poems. Given his comments throughout the lecture notes and in *The Book of American Negro Poetry*, it appears that Johnson wanted his students to understand the fullness of Dunbar's artistry. To help them do so, he provided evidence for his claims that the "poems in literary English" were more evocative of Dunbar's contribution to the New Negro era than were Dunbar's more popular dialect poems.

No simple advocacy of the "best" and most accepted English verse forms, Johnson's fifth lecture posited his readings of dialect more concretely. Johnson opened these notes with another critical distinction to clarify that dialect had artistic potential. "Conventional dialect," he wrote, was "a corruption of the English language used mainly for local color effect" (1). Stressing its use predominantly in crafting stereotypical depictions of African Americans, Johnson argued that it was possible to render the artistry of African Americans' oral forms without reliance on racial exaggeration. He then turned to his own poetry as an example, writing, "The effect here [in *God's Trombones* is] not to portray the old plantation preacher in his comic aspects—that had many times been done—but to interpret what was in his heart and mind, to give an art-governed expression to his utterance of the vision he had; at the same time retaining the movement, color, and unfettered imagination that was characteristic" (1). As the marginal note "selections from God's Trombones" following his explanation suggests, Johnson likely made his case by reciting and drawing his students' attention to passages such as "O Lord, we come this morning / Knee-bowed and body bent / Before thy throne of grace" from "Listen Lord: A Prayer" and these lines from "Go Down Death: A Funeral Sermon":

> Weep not, weep not,
> She is not dead;
> She's resting in the bosom of Jesus.
> Heart-broken husband—weep no more;
> Left-lonesome daughter—weep no more;
> She's only just gone home.[42]

The fourth and fifth lectures were representative of the "writer—text—reader—context" interplay that wove the series together. They also revealed Johnson's intention to model critical study of African American literature. Between them, Johnson employed close readings of his own work. His extended focus on dialect allowed him to identify and argue for it as a complex tool of racial representation. Johnson measured the artistry of Dunbar, at the time the most celebrated and popular African

American poet in America, through comparative analyses of Dunbar's poetry with that of the generation of poets constituting the Harlem Renaissance. The combination of these and other approaches supported his students' development from a basic to a more nuanced cultural literacy. Witnessing such passion and such biases from a celebrated African American poet likely enhanced their own reading experiences. Evidence for this outcome of Johnson's instruction emerges in the way the lecture notes document Johnson's interactions with his students.

In the last component of his notes, Johnson returned to the direct address that shaped his relationship with his readers. Early in his notes for the "Mandate Lecture," Johnson employed the phrase "for you" and indicated his willingness to honor his students' request for a survey of African American poets. In addition, he described in detail what he would not be able to address as a result of their "mandate," noting that he would have to forgo consideration of contemporary writers, black and white, other than poets, especially a "later group of Negro writers—the more or less Marxian group" (C). In addition, addressing his students, he acknowledged, "Your mandate also cuts out the brief references I intended to make regarding the contribution made by Negro Americans in the fields of invention, of scholarship, and scientific research" (D). Here again, the content that Johnson intended to constitute the final unit of the series advanced literary study as a historical and culturally relational exercise.

Despite this level of detail, the "Mandate Lecture" notes are an incomplete document in an ironic way. Whether they were lost or never included, absent from the "Mandate Lecture" are any indications of the components of the poets survey, selections from Johnson's own poetry, and the reflections on his own "creative processes" that his students had requested. Although they might have been more instructive for understanding how Johnson's students responded to the series, particularly why they requested these additions and what they may have read more generally, materials such as students' papers, class notes, and annotations in course texts are absent from Johnson's archived papers. Notwithstanding, Johnson's lecture notes provide insight into how his students practiced the critical cultural literacy—the instruction for being a New Negro reader—that English 123 fostered.

Pedagogy for Critical Readership

As he indicated at several places throughout his notes for the series, Johnson related to his students as an audience for whom a study of "the Negro in American literature" would be a challenge and a benefit. Fisk students had a high degree of racial awareness because of the activism that shaped the university during the 1930s, and the fact that they experienced Fisk during a period when it was solidifying the study of African American life and culture locally and nationally. As part of that experience, Johnson's lectures would have been a challenge for Fisk students because their prior education probably left them underprepared for the theoretical and practical insights he planned to offer. The lecture series and the coursework in the recitation sections of English 123 were important components in Fisk students' development into the civic leaders and cultural workers that the university desired them to become.

The list of paper topics that English 123 generated in spring 1933 sheds light on how Johnson's students responded to their preparation for these roles. For example, the fifth title on this list was "An Examination of British Writers in Their Attitude toward the Negro as Literary Material." Inasmuch as British writers constituted a (more) global context, this unidentified student's choice of topic suggests that Fisk students engaged in work that drew them outside the classroom and the United States. Other titles suggest an effort to study literature as a way to examine day-to-day occurrences in African American life, such as "The Attitude of the Negro Press toward Contemporary Negro Writers" and "Class Discriminations within the Negro Race as Shown in Negro Fiction."[43] As paper topics, these titles imply that Johnson's students in English 123 felt compelled to respond to his assertions from the inaugural lecture. Scott Zaluda has argued a similar point about the work of African American educators and their students during the Harlem Renaissance: "In recounting the institutionalization of African American studies, it is important to recognize that well before formal courses in African American history, society, and culture were being sanctioned for announcement in college catalogues, student writers had been working hard to produce a literature of African American contemporary life and history."[44]

Although the corresponding papers from spring semester 1933 were not archived, these titles point to the way African American literature circulated within black communication networks, and to the centrality of Harlem Renaissance writers to issues impacting black life. For example, even though the texts for English 123 did not include works on class such as E. Franklin Frazier's "La Bourgeoisie Noire," Franklin's perspectives were likely influential, given his presence at Fisk. As Eugene Levy has asserted, through English 123 Johnson "emphasized twentieth-century authors, beginning with Paul Laurence Dunbar and Charles Chesnutt and moving through writers of the Harlem Renaissance. He paid close attention to the background of contemporary writing, especially the historical circumstances that generated black American lifestyles. For black writers, Johnson obviously felt his Fisk students needed something more than the explication of literary texts."[45] One component of this "something more" was the opportunity to share his knowledge and model engaged reading of racial representation and recognition of artistry. Because he granted his students' request for a survey lecture, despite referring to it as a mandate, and included their paper titles in the course description that he crafted, Johnson clearly valued the ideas that his students brought with them to and voiced during English 123.

Johnson's move to Fisk University and an endowed professorship afforded him a new opportunity to focus his experiences as an artist-critic and further develop the production of prose, poetry, fiction, and drama among African Americans during the Harlem Renaissance into a literary tradition. My analysis of the extant materials from Fisk University's English 123, "The Negro in American Literature," points to the fashioning of a New Negro reader as the students and their teacher devised new ways to read and to write themselves into American culture.

EPILOGUE
On African American Writers and Readers

◊ ♦ ◊

In one compelling consideration of reading as a cultural practice, Susan Stewart has argued that "since the moment of Augustine's reading silently to himself, reading has inhabited the scenes of solitude: the attic, the beach, the commuter train, scenes whose profound loneliness arise only because of their proximity to a tumultuous life which remains outside their peripheries. The reader speaks only to the absent writer; the writer speaks only to the absent reader."[1]

To reflect on the relationship(s) between Harlem Renaissance writers and their African American readers using Stewart's instructive contention requires some revision. As a historic moment when reading and writing also reflected the complex, often difficult entry into and participation within a dynamic public culture for African Americans generally, the Harlem Renaissance fostered such relationships not only through dialogical absence but also, it is important to note, through dialogical presence. From the early 1920s through the mid-1930s especially, writers such as Sterling Brown, Gwendolyn Bennett, Countee Cullen, Jessie Fauset, and James Weldon Johnson envisioned and spoke to a New Negro reader in ways that made reading—as a cultural practice and an affirmation of racial identity—central to the Harlem Renaissance.

Far from solving "a dilemma of double audience" that Johnson described for the black writer in 1931, several writers asserted a dialogical presence within and through the period's print and literary cultures. That presence compelled public discussion, offered strategies for reading literature, and prompted readers to change their perspectives about the viability of literature and art as practices of racial uplift. As the foregoing chapters have demonstrated, Harlem Renaissance writers utilized newspapers, journals, and anthologies to cultivate New Negro readers. As a component of this outreach, they also urged other African Americans to attend readings and public lectures. Langston Hughes, for example, employed public readings of his poetry as one effort to reach out to African American readers and compel their attention. In the years when white readership for African American literature declined especially, Hughes focused his efforts on reaching as large a black audience as possible. In "Building a Black Audience in the 1930s: Langston Hughes, Poetry Readings, and the Golden Stair Press," Elizabeth Davey has argued that Hughes came to believe that "a mass black audience for black literature would be built through public readings, rather than private consumption of books."[2]

When Harlem Renaissance writers reflected on such face-to-face interactions with their African American readers, they affirmed their artistry and the value of the life experiences they depicted. Harlem Renaissance writers also recognized the agency of their African American readers. In a 1928 letter to Langston Hughes, Zora Neale Hurston wrote about her fieldwork in New Orleans, their collaboration, and their shared patron. She also requested more copies of Hughes's poetry, telling him: "The copy you autographed for me has done me lots of good. When I have to meet people in the group [of research subjects] & am asked to tell about myself—which I dont want to do for fear of saying that which I dont wish—I say I cant talk, but I'll read some verses from a Negro poet. You know these self-conscious Negroes are dynamite. Some are likely to object to my work so I can keep from explaining myself & still satisfy by talking about poets."[3]

Hurston's letter is a compelling record of how she maintained a degree of distance from but access to her research subjects by supporting Hughes's career as a poet. For Hurston, those "self-conscious Negroes" possessed a host of folklore worth documenting in their work songs, children's games, and love letters. In her letter to Hughes, she also pointed to the diverse group of African Americans who read and discussed literature, in this case poetry, throughout the period. Her observations underscore the myriad ways in which African Americans increasingly exhibited an identity as literate recipients of the period's flourishing culture. Not unlike features in the black press, literary anthologies, and the early literature course that this book chronicles, Hurston's letter is another record of how African America developed into the population of New Negro readers that so many Harlem Renaissance writers envisioned.

Today's writers read as African American or as reflecting African America similarly conceive of their writing as a conduit for reaching African American readers. Just as their Harlem Renaissance predecessors did, these writers invite dialogue with readers in print and in person. Their efforts perform a similar cultural work of moving readers to reflect on their identities in relation to the act of reading. I witnessed a palpable instance of this work in 2013 as author Daniel Black engaged with readers of his novel *Perfect Peace*.[4]

Composed of six men and six women who were members of the same predominantly African American church in Sanford, Florida, Bridging the Chapters and Lovers of Letters were two book clubs organized primarily as ways to socialize and enrich the bonds—religious, racial, and kin (a few of the members had grown up together)—that members shared. In deciding to feature the work of African American writers, book club members hoped to deepen their knowledge of African American literature while also addressing different but related experiences of being black in America. They decided to read *Perfect Peace* concurrently at the suggestion of one reader who was a member of both clubs; both groups graciously allowed me to attend the discussion.

Membership in each club involved suggesting works to read, and sometimes the book discussion included an opportunity to meet and speak with a given author. Bridging the Chapters, for example, has hosted other writers, including Nina Guilbeau (*Too Many Sisters*) and Clarence Reynolds (*Chatbox Manners*).[5] Members did not always have a personal connection to the authors whose work they read. But since Daniel Black had a prior connection with the joint member, the book discussion that ensued achieved a greater degree of intimacy than either Black or club members had previously experienced in such encounters. Indeed, although gaining insight into how and why Black had crafted specific plot twists formed a significant part of the discussion, members also shared several personal stories in appreciating his language use and storytelling, which they found evocative of familiar modes of expression.

As a chronicle of how a family is "forced to question everything they knew about gender, sexuality, unconditional love, and fulfillment," the idea for *Perfect Peace* originated "one day, in 2005, when I saw a child and couldn't determine if it was a boy or girl," Black explains in the reading group guide to his book.

> Then I wondered why it mattered at all. I knew the child was human; that wasn't up for question. But my desire to know lingered. I began to imagine the price the child was paying as the world sorted out its gender, or created one. My imagination ran free. I situated the story in the rural, segregated south in order to explore the specific ways in which southern black folk grapple with issues of gender, and I wanted to examine just how far a community is willing to go to "right" what they feel is wrong in one of its members. I also wanted to examine the ways in which patriarchy and homophobia have shaped the black community's constructs of God and salvation, leading its members to denounce and demean all in the name of something holy.[6]

Black's acknowledgment of his freedom to imagine and then depict such complexities of identity in "the rural, segregated south" and among "southern black folk" was an exercise of autonomy that he wanted readers of the novel to respect and accept.

The experience of reading a story in which a mother "tells her bewildered daughter, 'You was born a boy. I made you a girl. But that ain't what you was supposed to be. So from now on, you gon' be a boy. It'll be a little strange at first, but you'll get used to it, and this'll be over after a while' "[7] tested the members of Bridging the Chapters and Lovers of Letters. As their comments and dialogue with Black revealed, however, the book club members had experienced hardships just as the novel's characters did. Interspersed throughout their questions were also expressions of frustration with specific characters as well as affirmations of Black's abilities as a writer and his perspectives on his commitment to African American communities. One member confessed that reading *Perfect Peace* was difficult for her because of the pain it depicted. When she acknowledged that emotional pain was palpable among many people she knew, Black responded with an echo of his motivation to write for and about African Americans: "I think that there is much healing that we need to do in our communities. I see my work as a way to aid in that process."[8] Book club members followed his rejoinder with their own perspectives about the needs of their communities.

Witnessing this exchange as I developed *The Harlem Renaissance and the Idea of a New Negro Reader* helped me understand more tangibly the centrality of the historic relationship between African American writers and readers to African American literature, variously defined, and its operations. As the preceding chapters document, exchanges between Harlem Renaissance writers and African American readers, as well as those exchanges that Black and other African American writers have with their readers today, are evidence of that centrality. What is true for all contemporary writers is of course also true for writers such as Black: in terms of their own multiple identities as much as those of their readers, they are writing to, if not for, a more diverse literary audience. The reading publics that make up contemporary American society also read by way of an almost constant intermixture of print, digital, and oral platforms, which all contain elements of historic and complex practices of racial representation. This multimedia dynamic makes studying African American writers' roles as cultural literacy advocates as compelling as studying reading itself.

Notes

Introduction

1. "The New Negro Is Reading," *Half-Century Magazine* 6.5 (May 1919): 3, 16.
2. Ibid., 3.
3. St. Claire Drake and Horace Cayton, *Black Metropolis: A Study of Negro Life in a Northern City* (New York: Harcourt, Brace, 1945).
4. Howard A. Phelps, "Negro Life in Chicago," *Half-Century* 6.5 (May 1919): 12.
5. "The New Negro Is Reading," 15, 16. For *Half-Century*'s circulation and general aims, see Walter C. Daniels, *Black Journals of the United States* (Westport, Conn.: Greenwood Press, 1985), 195; and Noliwe M. Rooks, *Ladies' Pages: African American Women's Magazines and the Culture That Made Them* (New Brunswick: Rutgers University Press, 2004), 65–88.
6. Jessie Fauset, *There Is Confusion* (New York: Boni and Liveright, 1924); Countee Cullen, *Color* (New York: Harper and Brothers, 1925). *FIRE!! A Quarterly Devoted to Younger Negro Artists,* edited by Wallace Thurman, was published in 1926.
7. Statistical Abstract of the United States (Washington, D.C.: GPO, 1928), 27.
8. Patrick S. Washburn, *The African American Newspaper: Voice of Freedom* (Evanston: Northwestern University Press, 2006), 83.
9. Elizabeth Lindsay Davis, *Lifting as They Climb* (1933; repr., New York: G. K. Hall, 1996), 331.
10. Patricia Hill Collins, *Fighting Words: Black Women and the Search for Justice* (Minneapolis: University of Minnesota Press, 1998), 23.
11. Detroit Study Club, "Yearbook," 1926, 2, Detroit Study Club records, Burton Historical Collection, Detroit Public Library.
12. Victoria Wolcott, *Remaking Respectability: African American Women in Interwar Detroit* (Chapel Hill: University of North Carolina Press, 2001), 153.
13. Anne Meis Knupfer, *Toward a Tenderer Humanity and a Nobler Womanhood: African American Women's Clubs in Turn-of-the-Century Chicago* (New York: NYU Press, 1996), 122.
14. Catherine Squires, "The Black Press and the State: Attracting Unwanted (?) Attention," in *Counterpublics and the State,* ed. Robert Asen and Daniel Brouwer (New York: SUNY Press, 2001), 119. See Benedict Anderson, *Imagined Communities: Reflections of the Origin and Spread of Nationalism* (New York: Schocken, 1983).

15. Paul Laurence Dunbar, *Oak and Ivy* (Dayton: Press of United Brethren Publishing House, 1893); Pauline Hopkins, *Contending Forces: A Romance Illustrative of Negro Life North and South* (Boston: Colored Co-operative Publishing Company, 1900); James Weldon Johnson, *The Autobiography of an Ex-Coloured Man* (Boston: French & Company, 1912); Jean Toomer, *Cane* (New York: Boni and Liveright, 1923); Langston Hughes, *The Weary Blues* (New York: Knopf, 1926).
16. Charles Chesnutt, "The Negro in Books," in *Charles W. Chesnutt: Essays and Speeches*, ed. Joseph McElrath Jr., Robert Leitz, and Jesse Crisler (Stanford: Stanford University Press, 1999), 435–38.
17. Countee Cullen, "Yet Do I Marvel," in *Color* (New York: Harper & Brothers, 1925), 3.
18. Alain Locke, "The New Negro," in *The New Negro: An Interpretation* (New York: Albert and Charles Boni, 1925), 15.
19. Henry Louis Gates Jr., and Gene Andrew Jarrett, eds., *The New Negro: Readings on Race, Representation, and African American Culture, 1892–1938* (Princeton: Princeton University Press, 2007), 7. Examples of such scholarship include Paul Anderson, *Deep River: Music and Memory in Harlem Renaissance Thought* (Durham: Duke University Press, 2001); Geneviève Fabre and Michel Feith, eds., *Temples for Tomorrow: Looking Back at the Harlem Renaissance* (Bloomington: Indiana University Press, 2001); David Krasner, *A Beautiful Pageant: African American Theatre, Drama, and Performance in the Harlem Renaissance, 1910–1927* (New York: Palgrave Macmillan, 2002); A. B. Christa Schwartz, *Gay Voices of the Harlem Renaissance* (Bloomington: Indiana University Press, 2003); and Katherine Capshaw Smith, *Children's Literature of the Harlem Renaissance* (Bloomington: Indiana University Press, 2004).
20. Caroline Goeser, *Picturing the New Negro: Harlem Renaissance Print Culture and Modern Black Identity* (Lawrence: University Press of Kansas, 2007); James Danky, "Reading, Writing, and Resisting: African American Print Culture," in *A History of the Book in America*, vol. 4, *Print in Motion: The Expansion of Publishing and Reading in the United States, 1880–1940*, ed. Carl Kaestle and Janice Radway (Chapel Hill: University of North Carolina Press, 2009), 339–58; Leon Jackson, "The Talking Book and the Talking Book Historian: African American Cultures of Print—The State of the Discipline," *Book History* 13 (2010): 251–308.
21. Theodore Vincent, *Voices of a Black Nation: Political Journalism in the Harlem Renaissance* (Trenton: Africa World Press, 1973), 20; Abby Johnson and Ronald Johnson, *Propaganda and Aesthetics: The Literary Politics of Afro-American Magazines in the Twentieth Century* (Amherst: University of Massachusetts Press, 1979), xvii; Danky, "Reading, Writing, and Resisting," 340–41.
22. Carl Kaestle and Janice Radway, "A Framework for the History of Publishing and Reading in the United States, 1880–1940," in Kaestle and Radway, *A History of the Book in America*, 4:19.
23. Stanley Fish, *Is There a Text in This Class? The Authority of Interpretive Communities* (Cambridge: Harvard University Press, 1980), 171.
24. In *Art for Equality: The NAACP's Cultural Campaign for Civil Rights* (Lexington: University Press of Kentucky, 2014), Jenny Woodley argues, "It seems likely that the majority of [*Crisis*'s] readers were middle-class blacks (a reflection of the

membership of the NAACP itself at the time), who had the income, time, and inclination to read such a magazine, but that it was also known and discussed among a larger section of the African American community" (67).

25. Lara Langer Cohen and Jordan Alexander Stein, introduction to *Early African American Print Culture*, Material Texts series (Philadelphia: University of Pennsylvania Press, 2012), 15.
26. Jackson, "The Talking Book," 282.
27. Elizabeth McHenry, *Forgotten Readers: Recovering the Lost History of African American Literary Societies* (Durham: Duke University Press, 2002), 7.
28. Christine Pawley, "Seeking 'Significance': Actual Readers, Specific Reading Communities," *Book History* 5 (2002): 144.
29. Such records, even if extant, are difficult to acquire, as they are not catalogued but likely stored, unknown, in attics, closets, and other places within homes and institutions.
30. Davarian Baldwin, "New Negroes Forging a New World," in *Escape from New York: The New Negro Renaissance beyond Harlem*, ed. Davarian Baldwin and Minkah Makalani (Minneapolis: University of Minnesota Press, 2013), 19.
31. Fish, *Is There a Text*, 172.
32. Anderson, *Imagined Communities*, 6.
33. Molly Travis, *Reading Cultures: The Construction of Readers in the Twentieth Century* (Carbondale: Southern Illinois University Press, 1998), 13.
34. McHenry, *Forgotten Readers*, 19.
35. Karla Holloway, *BookMarks: Reading in Black and White* (New Brunswick: Rutgers University Press, 2006) 7.
36. W. E. B. Du Bois, "The Negro College," in *W. E. B. Du Bois: A Reader*, ed. David Levering Lewis (New York: Henry Holt, 1995), 72.
37. Michelle Phillips, "The Children of Double Consciousness: From *The Souls of Black Folk* to the Brownies' Book," *PMLA* 128.3 (May 2013): 593; Belinda Wheeler, introduction to "Gwendolyn Bennett's 'Ebony Flute,'" *PMLA* 128.3 (May 2013): 745.
38. Amy Jacques Garvey, "Read, Think, Then Talk," *Negro World* 17 (July 1926): 7.
39. Ibid.
40. In *Literary Garveyism: Garvey, Black Arts and the Harlem Renaissance* (Dover, Mass.: Majority Press, 1983), Tony Martin convincingly demonstrates how Garvey, through the *Negro World*, supported black literature for an international black readership: "Perhaps the most striking evidence of the rank and file literary activity came from the existence of literary clubs in many [UNIA] branches around the world. Two of the *Negro World*'s most prolific poets, J. R. Ralph Casimir of Dominica, West Indies[,] and Charles H. Este of Montreal, Canada, were leaders of their respective UNIA literary clubs. These clubs were following very much in the tradition, already noted, of Garvey's initial UNIA branch in Kingston, Jamaica. They arranged concerts and poetical readings, staged plays and held debates, often against non-UNIA literary clubs and debating societies. Literary clubs and similar activity were reported also from UNIA branches in Boston, Portland (Oregon), Santiago (Cuba), Norfolk and Newport News (Virginia), Philadelphia and New York among other places" (32). While the numbers of

readers are estimates, Garvey's *Negro World* attempted to encourage a pan-African or diasporan consciousness through readership.

41. Susannah Walker, *Style and Status: Selling Beauty to African American Women, 1920–1970* (Lexington: University Press of Kentucky, 2007), 15.
42. Sterling Brown, "Our Literary Audience," *Opportunity* 8.2 (February 1930): 42.
43. David Levering Lewis, introduction to *The Portable Harlem Renaissance Reader*, ed. David Levering Lewis (New York: Penguin Books, 1994), xxix.
44. Nathan Huggins, *The Harlem Renaissance* (New York: Oxford University Press, 1971), 64.
45. Richard Wright, "Blueprint for Negro Writing," *New Challenge* 2.2 (1937): 57.

1. Creating Critical Frameworks

1. Countee Cullen, "Dark Tower," *Opportunity* 4.48 (December 1926): 389.
2. Theodore Dreiser, *An American Tragedy* (New York: Boni and Liveright, 1925); Jessie Fauset, *There Is Confusion* (New York: Boni and Liveright, 1924); P. C. Wren, *Beau Geste* (New York: Grosset and Dunlap, 1926); Walter White, *Flight* (New York: Knopf, 1924); George Dorsey, *Why We Behave Like Human Beings* (New York: Harper & Brothers, 1925); and Alain Locke, *The New Negro: An Interpretation* (New York: Albert and Charles Boni, 1925). Popular literature during 1920s America also included genres such as "the Paul Bunyan legends and the cowboy ballads and such potential material as the desperados of the frontier and the show-boats of the rivers." Frederick Lewis Allen, *Only Yesterday: An Informal History of the 1920s* (New York: Harper Perennial, 2010), 243. Popular writers included Gene Stratton-Porter, Harold Bell Wright, and Zane Grey. Celebrated as they were in both the black and mainstream press and in African American book clubs, churches, and schools, Harlem Renaissance writers sought both popular and critical success.
3. Cullen, "Dark Tower," *Opportunity* 5.1 (January 1927): 24.
4. Ibid., 24.
5. Andreá Williams, *Dividing Lines: Class Anxiety and Postbellum Black Fiction* (Ann Arbor: University of Michigan Press, 2013), 2.
6. Sterling Brown, "Our Literary Audience," *Opportunity* 8.2 (February 1930): 61.
7. Angelyn Mitchell, *Within the Circle: An Anthology of African American Literary Criticism from the Harlem Renaissance to the Present* (Durham: Duke University Press, 1994), xxi.
8. James Smethurst, *The African American Roots of Modernism* (Chapel Hill: University of North Carolina Press, 2011), 150, 153.
9. Mark Jancovich, "The Southern New Critics," in *The Cambridge History of Literary Criticism: Modernism and the New Criticism*, ed. A. Walton Litz, Louis Menand, and Lawrence Rainey (Cambridge: Cambridge University Press, 2000), 200.
10. Robert Russ's "Chronology of the Harlem Renaissance" is one of several efforts that enable a measure of the period's print culture. His chronology, which covers the years 1917 through 1940, lists the titles of numerous anthologies. Victor Kramer and Robert Russ, eds., *Harlem Renaissance Re-examined: A Revised and Expanded Edition* (Troy, N.Y.: Whitston, 1997), 25–42.

11. James Weldon Johnson, preface to *The Book of American Negro Poetry*, 1st ed. (New York: Harcourt, Brace, & World, 1922), 40; hereafter cited by page in the text.
12. Louise Rosenblatt, *The Reader, the Text, the Poem: The Transactional Theory of the Literary Work* (Carbondale: Southern Illinois University Press, 1994), 25, 26.
13. Jessie Fauset, "As to Books," *Crisis* 24.2 (June 1922): 66.
14. Stanley Fish, *Is There a Text in This Class? The Authority of Interpretive Communities* (Cambridge: Harvard University Press, 1980), 48–49.
15. Georgia Douglas Johnson, "Race Authors in Dinner to Praise Jessie Fauset for New Novel on Negro," *Pittsburgh Courier*, March 29, 1924: 3.
16. Charles Flint Kellogg, *NAACP: A History of the National Association for the Advancement of Colored People*, vol. 1, *1909–1920* (Baltimore: Johns Hopkins University Press, 1967), 150.
17. Jessie Fauset, reviews of *Color* by Countee Cullen and *The Weary Blues* by Langston Hughes, "Our Book Shelf," *Crisis* 31.5 (March 1926): 238.
18. Michael Bibby, "The Disinterested and Fine: New Negro Renaissance Poetry and the Racial Formation of Modernist Studies," *Modernism/Modernity* 20.3 (September 2013): 497.
19. Fauset, "Our Book Shelf," 238; hereafter cited by page in the text.
20. Anne Carroll, "Protest and Affirmation: Composite and Texts in Crisis," *American Literature* 76.1 (March 2004): 89.
21. Kevin Young, "On Langston Hughes's *The Weary Blues*," Academy of American Poets, February 5, 2015, www.poets.org/poetsorg.
22. Cheryl Wall, " 'To tell the truth about us': The Fictions and Non-fictions of Jessie Fauset and Walter White," in *Cambridge Companion to the Harlem Renaissance*, ed. George Hutchinson (Cambridge: Cambridge University Press, 2007), 86.
23. James Smethurst, "Lyric Stars: Countee Cullen and Langston Hughes," ibid., 122.
24. "The Negro in Art: How Shall He Be Portrayed," *Crisis* 32.1 (June 1926): 71.
25. Katherine Capshaw Smith, *Children's Literature of the Harlem Renaissance* (Bloomington: Indiana University Press, 2004), xxi.
26. Brown, "Our Literary Audience," 42.
27. Georgia Douglas Johnson, *The Heart of a Woman* (Boston: The Cornhill Company, 1918); Claude McKay, *Harlem Shadows: The Poems of Claude McKay* (New York: Harcourt, Brace, and Company, 1922); Walter White, *The Fire in the Flint* (New York: Knopf, 1924).
28. Brown, "Our Literary Audience," 42; hereafter cited by page in the text.
29. James N. Comas, *Between Politics and Ethics: Toward a Vocative History of English Studies* (Carbondale: Southern Illinois University Press, 2006), 84.
30. W. Lawrence Hogue, *Discourse and the Other: The Production of the Afro-American Text* (Durham: Duke University Press, 1987), 7.
31. Sterling Brown, Arthur Davis, and Ulysses Lee, eds., *The Negro Caravan: Writings by American Negroes* (1941; repr., New York, Arno Press, 1969), 834.
32. Johnson, preface to *The Book of American Negro Poetry*, 41–42.
33. Brown, "Our Literary Audience," 44–45.
34. James Weldon Johnson, introduction to the first edition, reprinted in *The Collected Poems of Sterling A. Brown*, ed. Michael S. Harper (Chicago: TriQuarterly Press, 1989), 17.

35. Sterling Brown, *Outline for the Study of the Poetry of American Negroes* (New York: Harcourt, Brace, 1931).
36. Ibid., 18.
37. Sterling Brown, "Luck Is Fortune," *The Nation*, October 16, 1937, 409–10.
38. Ibid., 410.
39. Abby Johnson and Ronald Johnson, *Propaganda and Aesthetics: The Literary Politics of Afro-American Magazines in the Twentieth Century* (Amherst: University of Massachusetts Press, 1979), 101.
40. Alain Locke, foreword to Sterling Brown, *The Negro in American Fiction* (1937; repr., New York: Atheneum, 1969), n.p.; hereafter cited by page in the text.
41. Jessie Fauset, *There Is Confusion, Plum Bun* (London: Mathews & Marrot, 1928), *The Chinaberry Tree* (New York: Frederick A. Stokes, 1931), and *Comedy American Style* (New York: Frederick A. Stokes, 1933); Gertrude Sanborn, *Veiled Aristocrats* (New York: Associated Publishers, 1923); Nella Larsen, *Quicksand* (New York: Knopf, 1928); Geoffrey Barnes, *Dark Lustre* (New York: Alfred H. King, 1932); and Fannie Hurst, *Imitation of Life* (New York: P. F. Collier, 1934).
42. Joanne Gabbin, *Sterling A. Brown: Building the Black Aesthetic Tradition* (Charlottesville: University of Virginia Press, 1985), 193.
43. See, for example, Deborah McDowell, "The Neglected Dimension of Jessie Redmon Fauset," in *Conjuring: Black Women, Fiction, and Literary Tradition,* ed. Marjorie Pyrse and Hortense Spillers (Bloomington: Indiana University Press, 1985); and Kate Dossett, *Bridging Race Divides: Black Nationalism, Feminism, and Integration in the United States, 1896–1935* (Gainesville: University Press of Florida, 2008).
44. Gloria T. Hull, *Color, Sex, and Poetry: Three Women Writers of the Harlem Renaissance* (Bloomington: Indiana University Press, 1987); Cheryl Wall, *Women of the Harlem Renaissance* (Bloomington: Indiana University Press, 1995).
45. Gwendolyn Bennett, "To a Dark Girl," in *Caroling Dusk: An Anthology,* ed. Countee Cullen (1927; repr., New York: Citadel Press, 1993): 157; Angelina Grimké, *Rachel,* in *Selected Works of Angelina Weld Grimké,* ed. Carolivia Herron (Oxford: Oxford University Press, 1991); Zora Neale Hurston, "Sweat," in *Fire!! A Quarterly Devoted to Younger Negro Artists,* ed. Wallace Thurman (1926); and Larsen, *Quicksand.*

2. In Search of Black Writers (and Readers)

1. Nathan Huggins, *The Harlem Renaissance* (New York: Oxford University Press, 1971), 64–65.
2. Charles Johnson, "An Opportunity for Negro Writers," *Opportunity* 2.21 (September 1924): 258.
3. Mark Morrison, "Nationalism and the Modern American Canon," in *The Cambridge Companion to American Modernism,* ed. Walter Kalaidjian (Cambridge: Cambridge University Press, 2005), 26.
4. David Levering Lewis, *When Harlem Was in Vogue* (Oxford: Oxford University Press, 1989), 180.
5. Ibid., 98.

6. W. E. B. Du Bois, "Opinion of W. E. B. Du Bois: For a Prize Novel, $1000," *Crisis* 31.5 (March 1926): 217.
7. Charles Johnson, "The Last Warning," *Opportunity* 2.24 (December 1924): 355.
8. Abby Johnson and Ronald Johnson, *Propaganda and Aesthetics: The Literary Politics of Afro-American Magazines in the Twentieth Century* (Amherst: University of Massachusetts Press, 1979), 54.
9. Charles Johnson, "Editorials: One Year," *Opportunity* 2.13 (January 1924): 3.
10. Charles Johnson, "Editorials: We Begin a New Year," *Opportunity* 3.25 (January 1925): 2.
11. Charles Johnson, "A Note on the New Literary Movement," *Opportunity* 4.39 (March 1926): 80.
12. Charles Johnson, "Editorials: On Writing about Negroes," *Opportunity* 3.32 (August 1925): 227–28.
13. Johnson, "An Opportunity for Negro Writers," 258.
14. Ibid.
15. Ibid.
16. W. E. B. Du Bois, "Truth and Beauty," *Crisis* 25.1 (November 1922): 7.
17. W. E. B. Du Bois, "Criteria of Negro Art," *Crisis* 32.6 (October 1926): 296.
18. Du Bois, "Truth and Beauty," 7.
19. Langston Hughes, *The Big Sea* (1940; New York: Hill and Wang, 1993), 218.
20. W. E. B. Du Bois and Alain Locke, "The Younger Literary Movement," *Crisis* 27.4 (February 1924): 162.
21. Montgomery Gregory, "The Spirit of Phyllis Wheatley," *Opportunity* 2.18 (June 1924): 181.
22. George Schuyler, review of *There Is Confusion*, by Jessie Fauset, "New Books," *The Messenger* 6.5 (May 1924): 146.
23. Du Bois and Locke, "The Younger Literary Movement," 161.
24. "Notes on the New Books," *Crisis* 25.4 (February 1923): 161.
25. Montgomery Gregory, review of *Cane*, by Jean Toomer, "Our Book Shelf," *Opportunity* 1.12 (December 1923): 374, 375.
26. Gregory, "The Spirit of Phyllis Wheatley," 181.
27. Ibid., 182.
28. James Weldon Johnson, preface to *The Book of American Negro Poetry* (New York: Harcourt, Brace, 1922), 41.
29. "*Opportunity*'s Literary Prize Contest Awards," *Opportunity* 2.21 (September 1924): 277.
30. Ibid.
31. W. E. B. Du Bois, "Opinion of W. E. B. Du Bois: To Encourage Negro Art," *Crisis* 29.1 (November 1924): 11.
32. "The Amy E. Spingarn Prizes for Negro Literature and Art," *Crisis* 29.1 (November 1924): 24.
33. "Krigwa: CRISIS Prizes in Literature and Art, 1926," *Crisis* 33.2 (December 1926): 71.
34. "Krigwa Players Little Negro Theatre," *Crisis* 32.3 (July 1926): 134.
35. Jessie Fauset, "The Prize Story Competition," *Crisis* 26.2 (June 1923): 57–58.
36. Mark Seyboldt, "About the Short Story," *Crisis* 29.2 (December 1924): 79.

37. Ibid., 78, 79.
38. For another guest editorial by Mark Seyboldt, see "Play-Writing," *Crisis* 29.4 (February 1925): 164–65.
39. Charles Chesnutt to Du Bois, August 3, 1925, in *The Correspondence of W. E. B. Du Bois,* vol. 1, *Selections, 1877–1934,* ed. Herbert Aptheker (Amherst: University of Massachusetts Press, 1997), 316–17.
40. Ibid., 316.
41. Ibid., 317.
42. "Krigwa," *Crisis* 30.6 (October 1925): 276.
43. Ibid., 276, 278.
44. W. E. B. Du Bois, "Opinion of W. E. B. Du Bois: Krigwa, 1926," *Crisis* 31.3 (January 1926): 115.
45. Charles Johnson, "Editorials: The Judges and the Entries," *Opportunity* 4.42 (June 1926): 174.
46. Ibid.
47. Charles Johnson, "Editorials: New Patterns in Literature about the Negro," *Opportunity* 3.30 (June 1925): 164.
48. Johnson, "The Judges and the Entries," 174.
49. Charles Johnson, "Editorials: The Contest," *Opportunity* 3.34 (October 1925): 291.
50. Charles Johnson, "Editorials: The Opportunity Contest," *Opportunity* 5.9 (September 1927): 254.
51. Elizabeth Leonard, "Correspondence," *Crisis* 31.5 (March 1926): 218.
52. W. E. B. Du Bois, "Correspondence," *Crisis* 31.5 (March 1926): 218.
53. See David Levering Lewis's chapter "Crises at *Crisis*," in *W. E. B. Du Bois, 1868–1919: Biography of a Race* (New York: Owl Books, 1993), 466–500.
54. "The Outer Pocket," *Crisis* 33.1 (November 1926): 31.
55. Ibid., 31, 32.
56. Ethel C. Johnson, letter to the editor, "The Outer Pocket: Prize Stories," *Crisis* 34.2 (April 1927): 59.
57. W. E. B. Du Bois, "Opinion of W. E. B. Du Bois: A Questionnaire," *Crisis* 31.4 (February 1926): 165.
58. Johnson, "The Opportunity Contest," 254.
59. See, for example, Huggins, *The Harlem Renaissance;* George Hutchinson, *The Harlem Renaissance in Black and White* (Cambridge: Belknap Press, 1995); Johnson and Johnson, *Propaganda and Aesthetics;* and Lewis, *When Harlem Was in Vogue.*
60. "The Prize Winners," *Opportunity* 3.30 (June 1925): 186.
61. "Krigwa: CRISIS Prizes in Literature and Art, 1926," 71.
62. Ethel Pitts Walker, "Krigwa, a Theatre by, for, and about Black People," *Theatre Journal* 40.3 (October 1988): 353–54.
63. Johnson, "Editorials: The Contest," 292.
64. Charles Johnson, "Editorials: The Contest," *Opportunity* 3.29 (May 1925): 130–31.

3. Beyond *The New Negro*

1. "The Crisis Advertiser," *Crisis,* 28.1 (May 1924): 42, 41.
2. Ibid.; Carter G. Woodson, *The Negro in Our History* (Washington, D.C.: Associ-

ated Publishers, 1922); Robert T. Kerlin, *Negro Poets and Their Poems* (Washington, D.C.: Associated Publishers, 1923); and J. A. Rogers, *From "Superman" to Man* (Chicago: J. A. Rogers, 1917).
3. W. E. B. Du Bois, "Opinion of W. E. B. Du Bois: The Crisis Book Club," *Crisis* 27.3 (January 1924): 106.
4. Frank Horne, "Black Verse," *Opportunity* 2.23 (November 1924): 330; Newman Ivey White and Walter Clinton Jackson, *Anthology of Verse by American Negroes* (Durham: Trinity College Press, 1924).
5. Horne, "Black Verse," 330; Thomas W. Talley, ed., *Negro Folk Rhymes* (New York: Macmillan, 1922); and James Weldon Johnson, ed., *The Book of American Negro Poetry* (New York: Harcourt, Brace & World, 1922).
6. Arnold Rampersad, "The Book That Launched the Harlem Renaissance," *Journal of Blacks in Higher Education* 38 (Winter 2002–3): 87.
7. John Guillory, *Cultural Capital: The Problem of Literary Canon Formation* (Chicago: University of Chicago Press, 1993), 55.
8. With its preface "Negro Genius," Johnson's *Book of American Negro Poetry* made the practice standard.
9. Brent Hayes Edwards, *The Practice of Diaspora: Literature, Translation, and the Rise of Black Internationalism* (Cambridge: Harvard University Press, 2003), 44.
10. Among the period's literary anthologies are Alice Dunbar-Nelson, *Masterpieces in Negro Eloquence* (New York: The Bookery Publishing Company, 1914); Benjamin Brawley, *The Negro in Literature and Art in the United States* (New York: Duffield & Company, 1921); and Johnson, *Book of American Negro Poetry* (1922).
11. Alain Locke, foreword to *The New Negro* (1925; New York: Touchstone, 1997), xxv.
12. Ibid., xxvi.
13. William Braithwaite, "The Negro in American Literature," ibid., 44.
14. Alain Locke, "The New Negro," ibid., 3, 4–5; Langston Hughes, "Youth," ibid., 140; Alain Locke, "Negro Youth Speaks," ibid., 47.
15. Locke, "Negro Youth Speaks," 47.
16. Ibid., 48, 53.
17. John E. Bassett, *Harlem in Review* (Plainsboro, Pa.: Susquehanna University Press, 1992), 60–61.
18. Robert Bagnall, review of *The New Negro: An Interpretation*, edited by Alain Locke, "Our Book Shelf," *Opportunity* 4.38 (February 1926): 74.
19. W. E. B. Du Bois, review of *The New Negro: An Interpretation*, edited by Alain Locke, "Our Book Shelf," *Crisis* 31.3 (January 1926): 140.
20. W. E. B. Du Bois, *Darkwater: Voices from Within the Veil* (New York: Harcourt, Brace, and Howe, 1920); *The Philosophy and Opinions of Marcus Garvey*, ed. Amy Jacques Garvey (New York: Atheneum, 1923–1925); Georgia Douglas Johnson, *The Heart of a Woman* (Boston: The Cornhill Company, 1918); Johnson, *Book of American Negro Poetry*; Claude McKay, *Harlem Shadows: The Poems of Claude McKay* (New York: Harcourt, Brace, 1922); and Jean Toomer, *Cane* (New York: Boni and Liveright, 1923).
21. Du Bois, "Our Book Shelf," 141.
22. In a discussion of the changing realities and complexities of canons that informs my reading of *The New Negro*, Wendell Harris has argued that "the historical

resonance of a text (the degree to which it explicitly relates to other texts), the possible multiplication of its significances (the degree to which it is multivalent), the skill with which it is brought into the critical colloquy (the degree to which it finds fortunate sponsorship), and the congruence between its possible significances and critics' current preoccupations (the degree to which it proves malleable)—all these interact to determine how much interest the text can sustain over how long a period." Wendell Harris, "Canonicity," *PMLA* 106 (1991): 111. In terms of *The New Negro* specifically, Arnold Rampersad has addressed the multiple dynamics that construct its canonicity. For example, he noted that "in recent years, several of Locke's editorial decisions and predispositions, not to say prejudices, have been called into question by critics and scholars" ("The Book That Launched," 89–90). Barbara Foley has also offered a cogent analysis of Locke's editorial transformation of "Harlem: The Mecca of the Negro" into *The New Negro* and argued that Locke "was anxious to bury other debates," especially about leftist and radical politics. Barbara Foley, *Spectres of 1919: Class and Nation in the Making of the New Negro* (Urbana: University of Illinois Press, 2003), 233.
23. Du Bois, "Our Book Shelf," 141.
24. Locke, "Negro Youth Speaks," 51.
25. Locke, *The New Negro*, 134; Claude McKay, "The New Negro in Paris," in *The New Negro: Readings on Race, Representations, and African American Culture, 1892–1938*, ed. Henry Louis Gates Jr. and Gene Andrew Jarrett (Princeton: Princeton University Press, 2007), 145.
26. James Weldon Johnson, "The Dilemma of the Negro Author," *American Mercury* 15.60 (1928): 480.
27. Charles Johnson, ed., *Ebony and Topaz: A Collectanea* (New York: National Urban League, 1927), 11.
28. Richard Robbins, *Sidelines Activist: Charles S. Johnson and the Struggle for Civil Rights* (Jackson: University of Mississippi Press, 1996), 54.
29. Johnson, introduction to *Ebony and Topaz*, 11.
30. Locke, foreword to *The New Negro*, xxv.
31. Locke, "The New Negro," 11.
32. Johnson, *Ebony and Topaz*, 162.
33. Locke, "Negro Youth Speaks," 51, 50.
34. Johnson, *Ebony and Topaz*, 13.
35. Ibid., 12.
36. Locke, "The New Negro," 15.
37. Johnson, *Ebony and Topaz*, 11.
38. William Paulson reminds us that literary culture has a "penchant for assigning special value to language and its works. Wherever we find texts, reading, discourse, or linguistic structure serving as central preoccupations, controlling metaphors, or implicitly dominant models, we are (at least to some extent) in the presence of literary culture." William Paulson, *Literary Culture in a World Transformed: A Future for the Humanities* (Ithaca: Cornell University Press, 2001), 5.
39. Langston Hughes, "The Negro Artist and the Racial Mountain," *Nation* 122 (June 23, 1926): 693, 694.
40. Langston Hughes, "Dreamer," in Johnson, *Ebony and Topaz*, 36.

41. Johnson, ibid., 12.
42. W. E. B. Du Bois, "Criteria for Negro Art," *Crisis* 32.6 (October 1926): 296.
43. Countee Cullen, foreword to *Caroling Dusk: An Anthology* (1927; New York: Citadel Press, 1993), ix.
44. Countee Cullen, "The Dark Tower," *Opportunity* 6.6 (June 1928): 178.
45. Idella Purnell, review of *Caroling Dusk: An Anthology of Verse by Negro Poets*, "Our Book Shelf," *Opportunity* 5.12 (December 1927): 374.
46. Cullen, foreword to *Caroling Dusk*, xiv.
47. Anne Spencer, autobiographical note, ibid., 47.
48. Johnson, preface to *The Book of American Negro Poetry*, 21.
49. Claude McKay, autobiographical note in, *Caroling Dusk*, 82.
50. Ben Glaser, "Folk Iambics: Prosody, Vestiges, and Sterling Brown's *Outline for the Study of the Poetry of American Negroes*," *PMLA* 129.3 (May 2014): 423.
51. McKay, autobiographical note, 82.
52. W. E. B. Du Bois, "World of Color: The Negro Mind Reaches Out," in Locke, *The New Negro*, 397.
53. Nathan Huggins, *Harlem Renaissance* (New York: Oxford University Press, 1971), 30.
54. For a discussion of Cullen's critics, see Michael L. Lomax, "Countee Cullen: A Key to the Puzzle," in *Harlem Renaissance Re-examined: A Revised and Expanded Edition*, ed. Victor Kramer and Robert Russ (New York: Whitston, 1997), 239–48.
55. John Lash, "The Anthologist and the Negro Author," *Phylon* 8.1 (1947): 73.
56. Kenneth Kinnamon, "Anthologies of African-American Literature from 1845 to 1994," *Callaloo* 20.2 (1997): 467.
57. Cullen, foreword to *Caroling Dusk*, xii.
58. Ibid., xii–xiii.
59. Countee Cullen, "Yet Do I Marvel," in Johnson, *Book of American Negro Poetry*, 231.
60. Du Bois, "Criteria for Negro Art," 294.
61. Sterling Brown, "Our Literary Audience," *Opportunity* 8.2 (1930): 43.
62. Scott Zaluda, "Lost Voices of the Harlem Renaissance: Writing Assigned at Howard University, 1919–1931," *College Composition and Communication* 50.2 (1998): 247.
63. Mary Louise Strong, review of *Readings from Negro Authors for Schools and Colleges*, *Journal of Negro History* 17.3 (1932): 384.
64. Otelia Cromwell, Eva Dykes and Lorenzo Turner, eds., *Readings from Negro Authors for Schools and Colleges* (New York: Harcourt, 1931), iii.
65. See Alice Dunbar Nelson, "Negro Literature for Negro Pupils," *Southern Workman* 51.2 (February 1922): 59–63; and Charles Eaton Burch, "Freshman Papers in a Negro College," *Crisis* 22.5 (September 1921): 208, 210.
66. Cromwell, Dykes, and Turner, *Readings from Negro Authors*, iv.
67. The editors constituted a pioneering cohort of English and American literature scholars. Earning her degree in 1921 from Radcliffe College, Eva Beatrice Dykes became the first African American Ph.D. in English. The first African American graduate of Smith College, Otelia Cromwell was also the first African American woman to earn a degree, a doctorate, at Yale University, in 1926. Celebrated as the

first African American linguist, Lorenzo Dow Turner earned his doctorate from the University of Chicago the same year.
68. Cromwell, Dykes, and Tuner, *Readings from Negro Authors*, iv.
69. Ibid., 318–19.
70. Ibid., 319.
71. Ibid., 322.
72. Ibid., 320.
73. For a discussion of Cleanth Brooks's influence, see Lewis Simpson, ed., *The Possibilities of Order: Cleanth Brooks and His Work* (Baton Rouge: Louisiana State University Press, 1976).
74. W. E. B. Du Bois, *Souls of Black Folk* (1903; New York: Barnes and Noble Classics, 2003), 9.
75. Cromwell, Dykes, and Turner, *Readings from Negro Authors*, 342.
76. Alain Locke, "Our Little Renaissance," in *Ebony and Topaz*, 117.

4. Pedagogy for Critical Readership

1. James Weldon Johnson, *Along This Way: The Autobiography of James Weldon Johnson* (New York: Viking Press, 1933), 409.
2. Statistical Abstract of the United States: 1931 (Washington, D.C.: GPO, 1931), 5.
3. Joe Richardson, *A History of Fisk University, 1865–1946* (Montgomery: University of Alabama Press, 1980), 122, 129.
4. Christine Pawley, "Seeking 'Significance': Actual Readers, Specific Reading Communities," *Book History* 5 (2002): 149.
5. Richard Carroll, "Black Racial Spirit: An Analysis of James Weldon Johnson's Critical Perspective" *Phylon* 32.4 (1971): 345.
6. James Weldon Johnson, preface to the first edition of *The Book of American Negro Poetry* (New York: Harcourt, Brace, & World, 1922), 21.
7. John E. Bassett, *Harlem in Review: Critical Reactions to Black American Writers, 1917–1939* (Selinsgrove, Pa.: Susquehanna University Press, 1992), 85.
8. Johnson, preface to the first edition of *The Book of American Negro Poetry*, 41–42.
9. Ibid., 47.
10. James Weldon Johnson, "The Dilemma of the Negro Author," *American Mercury* 15.60 (1928): 477.
11. Ibid., 477, 478.
12. Ibid., 480.
13. Sterling Brown, "Our Literary Audience," *Opportunity* 8.2 (1930): 46.
14. Johnson, *Along This Way*, 238.
15. Johnson, "The Dilemma," 481.
16. Johnson, *Along This Way*, 129–30.
17. Ibid., 155.
18. Blyden Jackson, "A Postlude to a Renaissance," *Southern Review* 26.4 (1990): 752.
19. James Anderson, *The Education of Blacks in the South, 1860–1935* (Chapel Hill: University of North Carolina Press, 1988), 265.
20. Richardson, *A History of Fisk*, 89.

21. Eugene Levy, *James Weldon Johnson: Black Leader, Black Voice* (Chicago: University of Chicago Press, 1973), 291.
22. Marybeth Gasman and Edward Epstein, "Modern Art in the Old South: The Role of the Arts in Fisk University's Campus Curriculum," *Educational Researcher* 31.2 (2002): 13.
23. Henry Louis Gates Jr., "African American Criticism," in *Redrawing the Boundaries: The Transformation of English and American Literary Studies,* ed. Stephen Greenblatt and Giles Gunn (New York: Modern Language Association of America, 1992), 303.
24. Charles E. Burch, "Freshman Papers in a Negro College," *Crisis* 22.5 (September 1921): 209.
25. Scott Zaluda, "Lost Voices of the Harlem Renaissance: Writing Assigned at Howard University, 1919–1931," *College Composition and Communication* 50.2 (1998): 245.
26. James Weldon Johnson, "English 123—The Negro in American Literature," n.d., 1, James Weldon Johnson Papers, Beinecke Rare Book and Manuscript Library, Yale University, New Haven. The typed version of the course description for English 123, "The Negro in American Literature," appears on Fisk University letterhead stationery and includes a list of paper titles denoting "special subjects [that] are in some cases delivered before the class toward the close of the term." In listing the paper titles, Johnson indicated that the list was compiled from papers submitted during the spring of 1933. Johnson does not indicate here or in related ephemera why he prepared the course description. While the handwritten version is probably an early draft of the typed version, it does not include a date, as the typed version does. As a result, all references are to the typed version.
27. Ibid.
28. James Weldon Johnson, notes for "Inaugural Lecture" through "Lecture 7," n.d., 1, James Weldon Johnson Papers.
29. James Weldon Johnson, "Mandate Lecture," n.d., A, James Weldon Johnson Papers.
30. James Weldon Johnson, "Creative Genius Lecture," n.d., 3, James Weldon Johnson Papers.
31. Johnson, "The Dilemma," 481.
32. James Weldon Johnson, "Inaugural Lecture Notes" for English 123, n.d., 1, James Weldon Johnson Papers.
33. Gerald Graff has suggested that an important gauge of the status of American literature during this period was the 1928 publication of *The Reinterpretation of American Literature: Some Contributions toward the Understanding of Its Historical Development,* ed. Norman Foerster (New York: Harcourt, Brace, and Company). An illustration of the volume's focus is provided by Fred Lewis Pattee's "Call for a Literary Historian" (*Reinterpretation,* 3–22). Pattee was one of the founding members of the American Literature Group of the Modern Language Association. This 1924 *American Mercury* essay was reprinted in Foerster's volume to represent the group's belief that "a thoroughgoing historian must also be a critic" (*Reinterpretation,* xiv). Graff has argued, "The essays in the *Reinterpretation* did not oppose criticism to literary history but emphasized the need to

integrate the two, to merge history and criticism in a larger study that would bring literary studies into more intimate connection with American society." Gerald Graff, *Professing Literature: An Institutional History* (Chicago: University of Chicago Press, 1987), 214.

34. Carroll, "Black Racial Spirit," 345.
35. Johnson, "Inaugural Lecture Notes," 2–3. Hereafter, citations of Johnson's lecture notes will be given parenthetically in the text.
36. Johnson and Work, like noted bibliographers Alphonso Schomburg and Dorothy Porter, published and circulated bibliographies that were used by literary societies and schools, and among the general public in the United States and abroad. In doing so, they juxtaposed African, African American, and Afro-Caribbean textual production to mark the concurrent development of a cross-cultural and intra-racial literature. Given the ideology of status quo instruction still constraining African Americans' education during this time despite changes in leadership at a number of black schools and colleges, Johnson was probably aware that bibliographies such as Work's were underutilized or unknown. By making note of it, he made visible the body of work that would constitute the bulk of his students' study and allow them, at the outset of the course, to move beyond arguments that limited or denied the feasibility of studying black life and culture.
37. *Fisk University Bulletin* 6 (June 1931): 117.
38. Richardson, *History of Fisk University*, 141.
39. Kevin Gaines, *Uplifting the Race: Black Leadership, Politics, and Culture in the Twentieth Century* (Chapel Hill: University of North Carolina Press, 1996), xvii.
40. Richard Robbins, *Sidelines Activist: Charles S. Johnson and the Struggle for Civil Rights* (Jackson: University of Mississippi Press, 1996), 122.
41. Alice Dunbar-Nelson, "Negro Literature for Negro Pupils," *Southern Workman* 51.2 (1922): 563.
42. James Weldon Johnson, *God's Trombones* (New York: Viking, 1927), 13, 27.
43. Johnson, "English 123—The Negro in American Literature," 2.
44. Zaluda, "Lost Voices of the Harlem Renaissance," 246.
45. Levy, *James Weldon Johnson*, 325.

Epilogue

1. Susan Stewart, *On Longing: Narratives of the Miniature, the Gigantic, the Souvenir, the Collection* (Durham: Duke University Press, 1993), 14.
2. Elizabeth Davey, "Building a Black Audience in the 1930s: Langston Hughes, Poetry Readings, and the Golden Stair Press," in *Print Culture in a Diverse America*, ed. James P. Danky and Wayne Weigand (Urbana: University of Illinois Press, 1998), 224.
3. Carla Kaplan, ed., *Zora Neale Hurston: A Life in Letters* (New York: Doubleday, 2002), 125.
4. Daniel Black, *Perfect Peace* (New York: St. Martin's, 2010). I thank James Melton, Rene Akins, Daniel Black, and the members of Bridging the Chapters and Lovers of Letters of Sanford, Florida, for their welcome, warmth, and patience with my questions.

5. Nina Guilbeau, *Too Many Sisters* (Ocoee, Fla: Juania Books, 2008); and Clarence Reynolds, *Chatbox Manners: The Field Guide to Digital Etiquette* (Denver: Outskirts Press, 2011).
6. "Reading Group Guide: *Perfect Peace*," Macmillan Publishers website, n.d., http://us.macmillan.com/perfectpeace/DanielBlack.
7. Ibid.
8. Daniel Black, book club discussion, Bridging the Chapters and Lovers of Letters, Sanford, Fla., October 2013.

Index

African American press, 3, 4–5, 7, 27, 43, 98, 116; direct address in, 32–33, 56, 62, 66. *See also individual journals and newspapers*
Alexander, Lewis, 85
American Mercury, 97–98
American Negro Academy, 4
Anderson, Benedict, 4, 9
anthologies, 14, 21–22, 69–93, 129n10
Arnold, Matthew, 60, 83

Bagnall, Robert, 73
Baldwin, Davarian, 9
Barnes, Geoffrey, 39
Bennett, Gwendolyn, 10, 40, 115
Bibby, Michael, 28
Black, Daniel, 15, 117–19
Black Arts movement, 15
black women's club movement, 51
Bontemps, Arna, 101
book clubs, 3–4, 5, 33, 44, 123n40; *Perfect Peace* discussions, 15, 117–19
Booth, Wayne, 35
Boston Evening Transcript, 21
Bradstreet, Anne, 24–25
Braithwaite, William Stanley, 20–21, 39–40, 60–61, 72, 76, 89
Brown, Sterling, 12, 18, 32–41, 85, 87, 98, 102, 115; class issues, 20, 38–39; on dialect, 19, 36–38; Johnson on, 37 WORKS: *The Negro in American Fiction,* 38–40; *Opportunity* columns, 13, 32–33; "Our Literary Audience," 32–35, 37; *Southern Road,* 37

Browning, Elizabeth Barrett, 91
Browning, Robert, 4
Buck, Pearl, 51
Burch, Charles Eaton, 88, 102
Burns, Robert, 85, 109

cakewalk, 22
Carroll, Anne, 29
Carroll, Richard, 96, 105
Cayton, Horace, 2
Chesnutt, Charles, 5, 56–59, 103, 114
Chicago Defender, 11
class depictions, 19–20, 31–32, 38–40, 65
Cohen, Laura Langer, 8
Coleman, Anita Scott, 2
Crisis, 3, 8, 10–11, 13–14, 27–29, 42–67, 68, 102, 122n24; "The Crisis Advertiser," 68–69; contests, 13, 42–50, 52–67; "The Negro in Art" symposium, 31, 33, 63, 65
Cromwell, Otelia, 102, 131n67. See also *Readings from Negro Authors*
Cullen, Countee, 3, 34, 66, 73, 81–86, 115; Hughes on, 84 WORKS: *Caroling Dusk* (ed.), 71, 77, 81–86, 89, 92–93; *Color,* 3, 28–29; *Opportunity* columns, 16–18, 82, 85; "Yet Do I Marvel," 28, 86
Cunard, Nancy, 78

Danky, James, 7
Davey, Elizabeth, 116
Detroit Study Club, 3–4
dialect, 19, 36–38, 89; Brown on, 19, 36–38;

INDEX

dialect (*continued*)
  Chesnutt on, 58; in Dunbar, 19, 37, 85, 109; in Hughes, 29; Johnson on, 19, 24, 36–37, 109–11
Dorsey, George, 16
Drake, St. Clair, 2
Dreiser, Theodore, 16
Du Bois, W. E. B., 10, 50, 51, 76, 81, 83, 91, 103; *Crisis* editorship, 10, 13, 29, 42, 45, 46–50, 53, 54–55, 57–60, 62–67, 69, 74, 75 WORKS: "Criteria for Negro Art," 81, 86; *Darkwater*, 74; *The Souls of Black Folk*, 63
Dunbar, Paul Laurence, 5, 19, 37, 85, 90, 91; Johnson on, 109–10, 111–12, 114
Dunbar-Nelson, Alice, 88, 108
Dykes, Eva Beatrice, 102, 131n67. See also Readings from Negro Authors
education. *See* pedagogy

Edwards, Brent Hayes, 71
Eliot, T. S., 44

Faris, Ellsworth, 78
Fauset, Jessie, 4, 18, 35, 39–41, 71, 76, 115; Brown on, 20, 39–40; class issues, 20, 39–41; Cullen on, 85; editorial work, 27–28, 50, 55
  WORKS: *The Chinaberry Tree*, 39; *Comedy, American Style*, 39; *Crisis* reviews, 13, 26, 28–32, 33, 39, 51; *Plum Bun*, 39; *There Is Confusion*, 3, 16, 18, 27, 39, 40, 50–51, 52–53
FIRE!!, 3, 99
Fish, Stanley, 7–8
Fisher, Rudolph, 58–59, 64, 73
Fisk University, 14, 95–96, 99–101, 104–8, 113–14
Foley, Barbara, 130n22
folk life, 18–20, 35–41 passim, 55, 78–79, 80, 85
Frazier, E. Franklin, 114
Frost, Robert, 21, 60, 101
foundation support, 45
Frazier, E. Franklin, 66, 101

Gabbin, Joanne, 39
Gaines, Kevin, 107
Garvey, Amy Jacques, 11–12
Garvey, Marcus, 74, 123n40
Gates, Henry Louis, Jr., 6
genre distinctions, 18, 21–24, 56
Glaser, Ben, 83
Goeser, Caroline, 7
Graff, Gerald, 133n33
Gregory, Montgomery, 50–53
Grimké, Angelina Weld, 40, 90
Guilbeau, Nina, 117
Guillory, John, 70

Half-Century, 1–3, 11; "The New Negro Is Reading," 1, 3, 5
Harper, Frances, 26
Harris, Joel Chandler, 22
Harris, Wendell, 129n22
Hawthorne, Nathaniel, 56
Herskovitz, Melville, 78
Hill, Leslie Pinckney, 82
Hogue, Lawrence, 36
Holloway, Karla, 10
Holstein, Caspar, 45, 60
Hopkins, Pauline, 5
Horne, Frank, 69–70, 77
Horton, George, 26
Huggins, Nathan, 14, 43
Hughes, Langston, 50, 59–60, 71, 72, 74, 85, 99; Hurston and, 116; public readings, 116
  WORKS: "Dreamer," 80–81; "The Negro Artist and the Racial Mountain," 60, 79–80, 84; *The Weary Blues*, 5, 28, 29–31, 66; "Youth," 72
Hurst, Fanny, 39, 51
Hurston, Zora Neale, 4, 38, 40, 66, 99, 116–17

Jackson, Leon, 7, 8
Jancovich, Mark, 21
Jarrett, Gene Andrew, 6
Johnson, Abby and Ronald, 7, 46
Johnson, Charles S.: *Ebony and Topaz* anthology, 71, 77–81, 84, 89, 92–93;

INDEX

Fisk presidency, 101, 107; *Opportunity* editorship, 13, 43–44, 45–49, 53–54, 60–61, 65–67, 77
Johnson, Ethel, 64–65
Johnson, Fenton, 110
Johnson, Georgia Douglas, 21, 27, 33, 51, 74, 78, 90, 110
Johnson, Helene, 85
Johnson, James Weldon, 5, 18, 21–26, 32, 35, 41, 53, 60, 74, 85, 94–115, 134n36; Brown on, 36–38; class issues, 20; on dialect, 19, 24, 36–37, 109–11; teaching career, 14, 94–96, 99–114, 133n26
  WORKS: *Along This Way*, 94, 100, 105; *The Autobiography of an Ex-Coloured Man*, 98; *The Book of American Negro Poetry*, 13, 21–26, 36, 69, 74, 77, 81, 83, 96–97, 105, 110; "The Dilemma of the Negro Author," 97–99, 115; "Go Down Death," 111; *God's Trombones*, 111; "Lift Every Voice and Sing," 100
Johnson, Rosamond, 100
Jones, Thomas Elsa, 101

Kaestle, Carl, 7
Kerlin, Robert T., 69, 81
Kinnamon, Kenneth, 84
Krigwa little theater movement, 51, 55, 66

Larsen, Nella, 39, 40
Leonard, Elizabeth, 63
Levy, Eugene, 114
Lewis, David Levering, 45
Lewis, Sinclair, 58–59
literacy growth, 3
literary clubs. *See* book clubs
literary contests, 13–14, 33, 42–50, 67
Locke, Alain, 5–6, 14, 32, 50–51, 70–72, 75–76, 78–79, 86, 92, 130n22. *See also New Negro, The*
Lowell, Amy, 21

Martin, Tony, 123n40
McHenry, Elizabeth, 8, 10

McKay, Claude, 21, 33, 73, 74, 75, 83–84, 90, 97
McKenzie, Fayette A., 100–101
Mencken, H. L., 51
Messenger, The, 51
Micheaux, Oscar, 2
Miller, J. Hillis, 35
Morrison, Mark, 45

NAACP, 63, 101, 107, 123n24
National Association of Colored Women, 3
National Urban League, 3, 27, 40, 42, 47–48, 60, 71
Negro Caravan, 20, 36
Negro World, 3, 11–23, 123n40
Nelson, Alice Dunbar, 102
New Negro, The (Locke, ed.), 5–6, 8, 14, 16, 33, 70–79, 82, 83, 92, 129n22; Du Bois on, 74, 75
New Negro reader, 4, 10–11
Niagara movement, 51
Nugent, Richard Bruce, 99

O'Neill, Eugene, 34
Opportunity, 3, 10, 13–14, 16–17, 32, 40, 42–62, 65–67, 73; contests, 13, 42–48, 52–62, 65–67
Outline for the Study of the Poetry of American Negroes, 37–38
Overton, Anthony, 1
Ovington, Mary White, 58

Pattee, Fred Lewis, 133n33
Paulson, William, 130n38
Pawley, Christine, 8–9, 95
pedagogy, 86–90, 94–96, 99–114
Phelps, Howard A., 2
Phillips, Michelle, 10
Pittsburgh Courier, 13, 27
"Po' Boy" (song), 23–24, 37
Poe, Edgar Allan, 56
Porter, Dorothy, 134n36
Point du Sable, Jean Baptiste, 2
print culture, 6, 8–11, 13
Purnell, Idella, 82–83

INDEX

race relations institutes, 107
racial stereotypes, 19–20, 34, 40, 79–80, 98, 99, 110
racial uplift, 6, 9, 12, 15, 19–20, 27, 33–34, 96, 107, 116; anthologies and, 77–78, 87; literary contests and, 43, 44–45, 47, 54, 62, 66, 66
ragtime, 22–23
Radway, Janice, 7
Rampersad, Arnold, 70, 130n22
Readings from Negro Authors (Cromwell, Turner, Dykes, eds.), 71, 77, 86–93
Reinterpretation of American Literature, The (Foerster, ed.), 133n33
Reiss, Winold, 78
Reynolds, Clarence, 117
Richardson, Joe, 95
Rogers, J. A., 69
Roosevelt, Franklin D., 95
Rosenblatt, Louise, 23
Russ, Robert, 124n10

Sanborn, Gertrude, 39
Scarborough, Dorothy, 78
Schomburg, Alphonso, 134n36
Schuyler, George S., 51, 80
Seyboldt, Mark, 55–57
Shean, Edmund, 64
Smethurst, James, 20–21, 31
Smith, Katherine Capshaw, 32
Spence, Eulalie, 66
Spencer, Anne, 83, 97
Spingarn, Joel, 45, 59, 78
spirituals, 22–23, 24, 95
Squires, Catherine, 4
Stein, Jordan, 8
Stewart, Susan, 115
Stribling, T. S., 51
Strong, Mary Louise, 87
Stylus, 3

Survey Graphic, 71–72, 76
Synge, John Millington, 36, 97

Talley, Thomas W., 69
Thurman, Wallace, 78, 99
Toomer, Jean, 5, 45, 51–53, 73, 74, 89
Travis, Molly, 10
Turner, Lorenzo Dow, 101, 102, 131n67. *See also Readings from Negro Authors*

Vandercook, John W., 17–18
Van Vechten, Carl, 78
Vincent, Theodore, 7

Walker, A'Leila, 45
Walker, Susannah, 12
Washington, Booker T., 68
Weaver, John V. A., 85
Wells, H. G., 58
Wheatley, Phillis, 24–26
Wheeler, Belinda, 10
White, Newman Ivey, and Walter Clinton Jackson, 69–70, 81
White, Walter, 16, 33
white audiences, 5–6, 10, 97–98, 116
Whitman, Walt, 85
Williams, Andreá, 19
Williams, Lucy Ariel, 60
Williams-Irwin, Kathryn, 1
Wolcott, Victoria, 4
Woodley, Jenny, 122n24
Woodson, Carter G., 69
Work, Monroe, 106, 134n36
Wren, P. C., 16
Wright, Richard, 15

Young, Kevin, 30

Zaluda, Scott, 113

◊ ✦ ◊

Shawn Anthony Christian is associate professor of English and African American studies at Wheaton College. His work has appeared in *Wadabagei: A Journal of the Caribbean and Its Diasporas, CLA Journal, Pedagogy,* and in the volumes *Harlem Renaissance Revisited* and *Reading African American Experiences in the Obama Era.* He lives in Providence, Rhode Island.